My Four Husbands and Me

To Alice & Bob Yee,
In friendship always
6.24.07

Margaret Armatage

© Copyright 2003 Margaret Kathleen Armatage. All rights reserved.

No part of this publication may be reproduced, stored in a retrieval system, or transmitted, in any form or by any means, electronic, mechanical, photocopying, recording, or otherwise, without the written prior permission of the author.

Editor Elspeth Richmond
Cover design Roy Summerfield
Book design Maureen Salmon

Printed in Victoria, Canada

National Library of Canada Cataloguing in Publication Data

Armatage, Margaret Kathleen, 1918 -
My four husbands and me / Margaret Kathleen Armatage.
ISBN 1-55395-694-X
1. Armatage, Margaret Kathleen, 1918- 2. Greater Vancouver
(B.C.)--Biography. 3. Maine--Biography. I. Title.
FC3829.1.A74A3 2003 971.1'3304'092 C2003-900544-5
F1088.A74A3 2003

TRAFFORD

This book was published *on-demand* in cooperation with Trafford Publishing.
On-demand publishing is a unique process and service of making a book available for retail sale to the public taking advantage of on-demand manufacturing and Internet marketing. **On-demand publishing** includes promotions, retail sales, manufacturing, order fulfilment, accounting and collecting royalties on behalf of the author.

Suite 6E, 2333 Government St., Victoria, B.C. V8T 4P4, CANADA
Phone 250-383-6864 Toll-free 1-888-232-4444 (Canada & US)
Fax 250-383-6804 E-mail sales@trafford.com
Web site www.trafford.com TRAFFORD PUBLISHING IS A DIVISION OF TRAFFORD HOLDINGS LTD.
Trafford Catalogue #03-0057 www.trafford.com/robots/03-0057.html

10 9 8 7 6 5 4

Dedication

Dedicated to my sister, Elizabeth M. George and to my grandson by marriage, Sean Ewing, who suggested the title, and in memory of my niece, Jacqueline Sellentin, who kept at me to write this book and who gave me encouragement.

I also want to thank my friend, Nancy O'Carroll, for the help she gave me, Mary Rochford and Marcelle Horoupian for their support. Joy Bond, of Invermere, provided pictures of our home and family as well as information about my mother's death. My grateful thanks to her, also, and to my good and wonderful friend, Roy Summerfield, for his unfailing help.

Contents

Foreword

I am proud to say I have been a friend of Margaret Armatage for more than 25 years, or, according to the title of her book, since husband number two, Ted Thompson. I first met her when I accepted a vice president's position at a regional campus of the University of Maine in Presque Isle. When I arrived early in October in need of housing, the president of the University suggested I contact a couple who went to Florida for the winter and who might need a house sitter. Within a few hours, I had a place to stay and a lifelong friend.

Margaret and Ted invited me to stay with them for a month or so before they actually left. As Margaret has always risen early, I was soon the recipient of a freshly prepared breakfast and warm conversation every morning. In a short time, I discovered that Margaret was a sort of Renaissance person who is active all day and who mastered everything she attempted from golf to gardening and landscaping to interior design. I also learned that Margaret had overcome considerable adversity in her early life and had adapted well, although at times not easily, to a whole new social environment, from a life in the Canadian frontier to that of a busy socialite in a northern New England culture.

The first thing I learned on my own in Northern Maine was not to be prejudiced about the stereotypes of New Englanders being distant, if not laconic. I found I could be myself and that I was easily accepted on that basis. Margaret followed the same precept, but had to earn some acceptance. She had come to Northern Maine as a self-made, successful woman entrepreneur, which would earn deep respect and lots of attention. She had also entered a social elite group that included her new husband. Ted Thompson and his first wife had three children, who became, for the most part, a joy to Margaret. Some locals, however, resisted the opportunity to reach out to Margaret though Ted's previous marriage had ended very unhappily five years earlier with no chance of reconciliation.

Margaret had worked hard since childhood to earn everything she ever had, from a night's meal to financial independence. She had known plenty of good people and a few really bad actors. Unlike most people, she can quickly tell the difference between a good person and a bad person. It hurt her feelings that some people took a great deal of time before accepting her, but most eventually did accept her generously and appreciated all the new skills and energy she brought to the community. Some confessed privately their own hurt at being talked about unkindly or unfairly.

Margaret has never taken a whole lot of time to look back and second guess herself or others, and that quality sustained her during her arrival in Maine. It has never let her down. I would characterize people who are active and successful through effort and struggle as having an internal compass that always points true north. Trivial distractions seldom deter this type of individual, and something fleeting like a social slight is like a mosquito bite to a girl who grew up in the wilderness of Canada.

I should add that Margaret's ability to distinguish between good and bad people also applies to her marriages, with two uncharacteristically brief interludes. The first occurred when she was young and had not yet learned to accept her own judgment; the second when she was on the rebound from Ted Thompson's tragic death from cancer.

Her relationships with Ted Thompson and Colin Armatage (husband number four) were marriages made in heaven, with both partners ideally suited to one another. Ted was an avid outdoorsman, yet cultivated in all the social graces. Margaret had learned etiquette and style on her own and was equally comfortable in formal or casual situations. Ted and Margaret's was a marriage in which each tried to keep up with the other so as not to be left out of any fun. Colin was a very creative person, who was a first rate partner to Margaret's gardening and travel interests and who kept a beautiful photographic record of all they did together. Ted was an extrovert who was able to make a quick study of anything. Colin was more of an introvert. He would take his time analyzing things without a priori judgment. Both were sweet and caring husbands, attentive hosts and special people. I was fortunate to spend quality time with both and was very happy that Margaret met both of them. I cannot recall what Colin told me of his first impressions of Margaret. I know that they met through the recommendation of mutual friends, who seemed to share Margaret's keen insights about people. I was privileged during a recent visit with Margaret to read excerpts of an extraordinary diary written by Ted Thompson. It is clear that he had several twinkles in his eyes after his first meeting with Margaret.

When Margaret told me she was writing an autobiography, I was very excited. I was happy as her friend because I knew it would be a project that would energize her, and it has. I was also happy because I know it to be the record of a woman who made it through difficult and tragic times, who never cursed the darkness and who could offer hope and inspiration to young and old about lives lived to the fullest.

Margaret Armatage is an individual with an incredible work ethic who, like Benjamin Franklin, is 'early to bed and early to rise,' with everything in between at full throttle with maximum effectiveness and efficiency. Any bumps in the road are quickly dealt with and forgotten. She lives in a cosmopolitan world, with many dear friends from diverse backgrounds. She is a master of many tasks (I should not overlook painting, which she also taught herself), and would have been successful at many more. She is an individual who would have benefited enormously from a higher education but who has not missed a beat of life without it.

I commend her book because it shows by example what a young woman with a good heart, an inquisitive mind and a good work ethic based on perseverance and resilience can do in a free society. Margaret could have written a 'been there, done that' kind of book. That would have made her more of a judge and critic, rather than an exemplar. She chose to share, instead what is most inspiring, how she arrived at where she is today. She is happy. She is renewed with each day's activities. She has no complaints about her fate. What one learns from her examined life is that one has to live one's own life to his/her natural conclusions, and that beautiful fairy tales are all around us waiting to be scripted.

Dennis E. Donham

Friend

Franklin Park, PA

USA

Introduction

I have been married four times. I guess you could say I am extraordinarily optimistic, unusually lucky, and willing to gamble on things turning out for the best. On the other hand, some people might suggest that I've been somewhat foolhardy in my life and paid the price for taking more chances than most women would. I've been both rich and dirt poor. I've seen much of the world and stayed in the best hotels. I've had bed bug bites. I owned a successful business and built a lovely home and two cottage retreats. I've worn designer clothes but once wondered where I'd find the money for a new pair of shoes. I can still use a hammer, scrub floors and prune trees in my garden. I've never owned any car but a Cadillac and, at 84, I drive one today. There has always been a man in my life, and sometimes more than one at a time. I have loved two men with all my heart.

Chapter 1

Childhood

I took the picture out and looked at it, as I had done countless times. I am just sixteen in the photograph. It is what people called 'calendar art', the sort of picture found hanging on the walls in service station offices and mechanic shops not so long ago. I am nude.

"Scandalous!" our parents would have said. Never a prude, I was proud of my body and yet I kept the picture hidden. Hidden for over sixty years, the photograph reminds me just about how far I've come since that warm summer afternoon on the Fraser River when I posed for it. It also reminds me of the struggles ahead of my sister Betty and me when our mother died. Betty was a toddler then, and I was just a few days old. She was my big sister, the wise one, the leader. I followed where her footsteps took me. Now our roles are reversed. I am the one who remembers and she follows me because her memories are lost forever.

I came into this world just a few short days before the First World War ended. I was born either November the second or fourth, 1918. I never knew my mother. She died when I was six weeks old during the terrible

Spanish influenza epidemic, which began in 1917 and raged until 1918. It reached our little valley community of Invermere soon after I was born. The strange thing about that epidemic was that it struck down young, healthy people. Many families, like ours, were left without a parent. Coming as it did, right at the end of a war that had already taken the lives of thousands of young men, it was a cruel blow.

I cherish the only picture I have of my mother–she was a beautiful woman, with thick, lustrous hair piled high on her head in the Gibson girl fashion of the day. My father named me Margaret, in her memory. I often looked at her picture and wondered what she was like.

It was a very difficult time for my father. Like the many immigrants who left England to seek prosperity early in the last century, he had high hopes of success in Canada. Most of these newcomers were enticed by stories of free land and a chance to make a fortune in an undeveloped and uncrowded new country. Many men were second sons of prosperous families, unlikely to inherit the family wealth. The luckiest of them were known as remittance men, sent off with the promise of a monthly stipend. Many of them, like my

My mother, Kathleen Margaret Coles.

parents, were disillusioned with the realities of a harsh climate and lack of resources to cope with the many challenges of resettlement. Father's family had been prosperous, but those days were gone forever when he set off for a new life in Canada.

Father cleared the land for a small farm in Invermere, B.C., where he was trying to start a freight transfer business between Athlamer and Golden. It looked as if there would soon be a good market for agricultural produce and he saw a niche in the transportation business for moving those products from farm to market. Our log home was a proud testament to his skill as a builder.

In 1914, our mother, homesick for the old country, proudly took her baby son, Jack, home to her family in England. She hurried home to my father on a sister ship to the Lusitania after the First World War broke out. As she boarded the train in Quebec City for the long journey across the country, she must have been very grateful to have made the dangerous Atlantic crossing safely. I

Our home in Invermere; Mother and babies.

Above: Father and we three children.
Left: Jack, Betty and my mother.

wonder what she was thinking as the train crossed the country, the rocky scrub lands of Northern Ontario, the wide prairies, and then through the Rockies. Life in her adopted land was so different from her life in the lovely English town of Windsor. Was she homesick or did she return eagerly to her new husband and her cozy home near the banks of beautiful Lake Windermere? Just four years later she was dead, buried in the small cemetery there.

Jack and me.

My brother, John Alfred (Jack) was five years old. Betty, our sister was two. I was the new baby. At last, everything seemed poised in father's life to make all his dreams of success in his adopted land come true.

Now my father was alone with two small children and a baby. An aunt came from England to care for us soon after the tragedy occurred, but father soon could see that our little family needed a mother. Within two years he married the nurse who assisted with my birth. Their wedding picture shows them a prosperous and stylish couple surrounded by local friends.

Above: The wedding party in our garden.
Left: Father and our stepmother on their wedding day.

In another picture taken at that time, I am a plump, little curly headed blond girl, already my father's favourite. Betty was also fair but stockier and even then had broad shoulders. She was very athletic and how I envied her ability to turn cartwheels effortlessly, do handstands and chin herself on the branches of the trees in our yard! Try as I might, I could never do any of those things but later took up basketball and badminton to compensate for my lack as a gymnast. In another picture, Jack's mischievous smile masks the face of a difficult and unhappy boy.

An aunt came from England when Mother died.

Our stepmother, Anne Letts, was an English woman, a member of the Victorian Order of Nurses, who was nursing in Halifax when a munitions ship blew up, killing over a thousand people and injuring many more. "It was terrible!" she often told us. "Bodies everywhere, shoes here and there, the silhouette of a man's body where he had been blown through a window." Beautiful Invermere, nestled in the Columbia Valley, between the Rockies and the Purcell mountains was a safe haven after the horror she had witnessed.

Left: My stepmother in her V.O.N. uniform.

Right: Anne Letts in her vaudeville days.

When I think of Invermere now, I remember all the beautiful wildflowers. My sister used to say, "When we took you to school in a buggy, you were a real nuisance. You wanted each and every flower along the way and nothing would do but we had to stop and pick this one and that one until your arms were filled with them." I still love flowers to this day. Perhaps that was when my love of gardening was born.

One of my first memories is of my brother Jack playing with matches and setting fire to the straw outside our barn. Betty and I were terrified. Even at my age, I knew that matches were dangerous. They were kept in a tin on a shelf over the stove. We knew better than to touch them. Father was away but a neighbour, passing by in a democrat, managed to put the flames out. Dad was furious with my brother. Fire in the valley was terribly dangerous. The wind could sweep down the valley spreading the flames in lightning quick time. Of course there was no fire department, only the 'bucket brigade'.

Jack was always into one kind of trouble or another. There was a wood box at the side of the house and it was Jack's chore to fill it. He never did it until Dad got angry. Another time, Jack tried to stop the chickens from running away by tying strings around their necks and then tying them to the fence. When father heard all the squawking, Jack was in trouble again. It didn't help that Jack was an unhappy, sulky boy much of the time. Only much later did I realize that Jack missed our mother and resented our stepmother. He had been the centre of our mother's attention, especially when she took him back to England. Now she was gone and our stepmother was busy raising the three of us as well as doing all the hard physical labour entailed in managing the homestead. And far from being companions, Betty and I were just a couple of nuisances to him. Today, we understand that children go through a natural grieving process when a parent dies. Back then, even children were expected to hide their grief. I guess Jack hid his in naughtiness. I believe now that he never got over our mother's death. Father, of the old British school of the stiff upper lip, was not likely to comfort him. Our stepmother didn't know how to handle him either. A ready-made family with an unhappy boy and two lively toddlers must have been a challenge for her.

Father in his democrat.

Sometimes, though, even father had to laugh at Jack's pranks. As a boy, he got into his own kind of mischief. He told us once how he and a friend had climbed a garden wall for a peek at a girl they liked. In scrambling down, he lost one of his shoes. The girl's father caught them and both boys were beaten. Just the same, our father could be a stern man who thought the discipline he had received had done him no harm. If Jack misbehaved, father's punishment was swift.

Betty and I learned to put the unhappy scenes with Jack out of our minds. We often heard our stepmother say, "Be like the sundial. Count only the sunny hours," and we did have many.

I remember my parents making ice cream in a churn filled with rock salt. Somehow the salt spilled over on to the lawn and killed much of the grass. I also recall being in the barn at milking time and seeing father squirt the warm milk into the eager, open mouths of the barn cats.

We had both cows and horses. When Betty and I returned in 1939, the homestead was just as I remembered. I understood then how my father must have known when we left that beautiful valley, that his dreams of being a successful gentleman farmer with a thriving transport business would never be realized.

Our stepmother was never very well and, thinking back, I realize that she was not very happy in Invermere. I think the high altitude did not suit her and, in spite of her terrible experience in Halifax, perhaps she never lost her love of cities. She was older than my father and had been an amateur actress at one time. She may have been lonely too, because father sold the farm and we moved to New Westminster where she had a friend. We knew that Father didn't want to leave our beautiful valley.

I can never forget standing beside him in our empty house after all our belongings had been loaded onto our truck. It was so quiet, standing there. Then suddenly father gave my hand a squeeze and said, "Well, little missy, onward and upward! Let's go!"

It was a long trip for a little girl to the 'Royal City' of New Westminster. Our covered truck was crammed tightly with everything we owned. There was just enough room left for us to sleep in it when we stopped at night. We each had our own little mattress and loved camping in the truck each night. We could look out at the stars, sometimes hear the coyotes and imagine we were

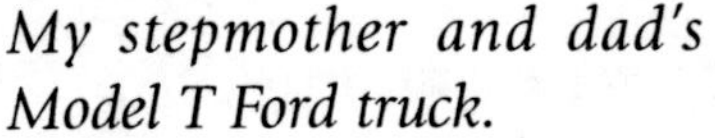

My stepmother and dad's Model T Ford truck.

Our Model T Ford under a bridge.

pioneers travelling in covered wagons. It was an adventure. For a few days we lived like gypsies.

Once we 'lost' pots and pans out of the back of the truck and called to father, "Stop!" The engine made so much noise that he didn't hear us. We banged our fists on the cab until he brought the truck to a stop, pulled over and we all clambered out to collect our pots. I think he suspected we helped the pots tumble out. Jack was certainly capable of mischief, but father and mother were light-hearted enough on that trip to play along with our game.

"Mind you don't let anything else fall out!" father warned.

For once, we were carefree. That's when I learned that you can have fun even if times are tough and you don't have much money. We each took turns sitting up front with mother and father, but to tell the truth, we children liked it best in the back. Even Jack lost his sulkiness on this new adventure. It was harvest time and, along the way, some good people gave us watermelons, cantaloupes and tomatoes as we travelled down into Washington State on our way to New Westminster.

Auntie Theda, as we called my mother's friend, rented a place for us in New Westminster. The first night, mother was horrified to discover bed bugs on the mattress covers. You can be sure that she moved us out of there in a hurry. We even had to burn some of our clothes. We moved again several times before father finally bought a lot in the West End of town and started, once again, to build a home for us. Probably because he was such a meticulous craftsperson, it seemed to take him forever to finish the little house at 1718 Dublin Street. Betty and I both looked forward to having our own rooms, upstairs, looking down into the garden below, so every day we hurried over to see how he was progressing. There was a cozy little parlour, a bright kitchen and four bedrooms. From the back of the house, we looked down at the broad Fraser River below us.

Father, our stepmother, Anne, Aunt Theda, Jack, Betty and Margaret.

"Now don't you children ever think of swimming in that river," father warned. "There's a mighty strong current and you'd be pulled down and out to the Pacific Ocean before you could say, "Bob's your uncle!"

Bush surrounded our house in the 1920's. Every day we followed a long trail through the woods to Lord Kelvin School. The other kids at the school made fun of our English accents and of the clothes mother insisted we wear. Auntie LaBelle, another of mother's friends, gave us new clothes and, although she was single and had no children of her own, she somehow knew what the other children wore to school. She understood also, how being different would make it much harder for us to be accepted. Mother, though, wouldn't let us wear our new clothes to school. She said we must save the new clothes for church on Sunday. We had a fort in the bush on the way to school, so we kept an old trunk there with our new clothes and changed into them after we left the house every morning. Of course, we also had to remember to change back again after school each day, too. Now I wonder how it was that mother never once noticed our good clothes were missing from our closets. Betty and I were always afraid she would find out and tell father what we had done.

Eventually, mother did discover our little scheme. One day she unexpectedly came to school to see Jack's teacher, and saw us in our best dresses. She was not angry, but listened quietly as we told her how the other girls made fun of our clothes. "Why didn't you tell me?" she asked.

I was no scholar. I liked to have a good time and didn't take school seriously. Even so, I once won first prize in a story writing contest. I had a good imagination. Nevertheless, I dreaded report card time because both

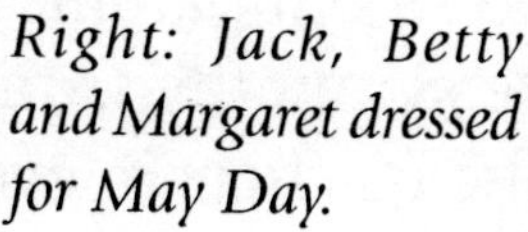

Left: Jack, Margaret, Betty Sellentin.

Right: Jack, Betty and Margaret dressed for May Day.

our parents expected us to do well at school. My report card was usually unsatisfactory.

"Margaret talks too much," one teacher wrote. "She should socialize less and concentrate more."

"Margaret needs to pay more attention during class" wrote another. "She daydreams."

"Margaret needs to spend more time on arithmetic and spelling."

Betty once signed mother's name on my report card so our parents would not see my bad marks. When our parents discovered our forgery, the two of us got the strap, both at school and at home.

I tried not to attract the teacher's attention in class but sometimes trouble just seemed to seek me out. One day I explained to the teacher that I couldn't see the blackboard. She called me up to the front of the class and shoved my nose up against the board. "Now, can you see?" she demanded roughly. This same teacher threw another girl down the aisle. If we needed to leave the room to go to the bathroom she made us put one hand up for #1 and both hands up for #2. We never questioned anything the teacher did and, of course, we knew better that to tell our parents any of this. It was no use trying to evoke sympathy from them. Mother and father supported the teachers in everything they did.

Of the two of us, Betty was always the better student. She had to be the best, while I was content to be in the middle of the class. She was a good speller and could paint well, too. She was my best friend, but I have to admit, sometimes she was jealous of me. Once, when I received both a badminton set and paints for my birthday, she said, "Mother always spoils you!"

Still, I enjoyed the classes most of the time, especially home economics. Every girl had a sewing machine and we learned to cook and to set a table properly. We also learned cooking at home. Mother was a good teacher too, and taught us how to cook and knit. When we helped her make pies Betty was always cross with me for eating the raw pastry. While I've lost my taste for dough, I love to make a good pie for my friends to this day. What a comfort is it to see a freshly baked, lattice-topped pie made with freshly-picked, ripe Okanagan cherries on the kitchen counter! At 84, I still do all my own cooking and entertaining.

Father tried all kinds of ways to make a living. He was so determined to be successful and recoup the losses of his once wealthy family back in England. The struggle would kill him and leave us in poverty. He even had shares in the Paradise Gold mine, hoping to strike it rich. Then he tried mining for a gypsum company in Falkland, B.C. Finally he returned to New Westminster to start a workshop at home. Before long, we were all involved in this enterprise. We would cut up the gypsum into little squares, sand them on a wheel and wrap them up as samples to send all over Canada. Now, there are stringent rules for the handling and packing of gypsum. Special gloves and masks are required and, of course, children would never be allowed to do such work. But this was the beginning of the 'Dirty Thirties' and within a few short years, Betty and I found ourselves wishing we could still earn a few dollars this way.

After breathing in the gypsum at the mine and then in our workshop, father's lungs were damaged and the doctor told him he had to work in the fresh air. That was when he started building fishponds for people and raising gold fish.

Father used to say, "Keep an eye out for a rabbit, now! It's good luck if you see one first thing in the morning." I don't remember seeing many rabbits in those days but our luck seemed to have taken a turn for the better. They were good years then, when I was nine. Father was a knowledgeable gardener and, just as mother taught us to cook and sew, father taught us to love gardening. Jack, Betty and I had our own little gardens and I still remember the botanical plant names he taught us so patiently. We also had raspberry canes and we sold goldfish and garden plants in a stall at the New Westminster Market.

Church bells called us every Sunday to Holy Trinity Cathedral, a beautiful stone church modeled on St. Paul's church in Kensington. It is quite likely that both father and mother were familiar with St. Paul's and felt at home in Holy Trinity for that reason. They were excellent singers and sang in the church choir. I don't recall that the church had Sunday school. Our parents expected us to sit quietly through the service which was no trouble for me. My eyes would droop and I was soon fast asleep. Betty often had to wake me up when the sermon ended. The delicious smell of the pork roast, that mother put in the oven before we left for church, greeted us when we returned home. We always had a good dinner with vegetables from our garden and a special dessert such as tapioca pudding, one of my favourites even now.

Betty and I received our confirmation at Holy Trinity. I really don't remember much about the ceremony except that both of parents were there and Auntie LaBelle bought our lovely white dresses and our veils. As I still find comfort in the services, music and liturgy of the Anglican Church, I guess you could say I was firmly confirmed!

Our stepmother lovingly took good care of us, teaching us, even though she was not a fastidious housekeeper, that "Cleanliness is next to Godliness," and watching over us while Betty and I brushed our hair 100 times each night at bedtime. We always said grace before every meal. "O Lord, ever mindful of the needs of others, bless this food to Thy use and us to Thy service."

We had to clean our plates at every meal. "Think of the starving Armenians," mother said. "They would be very happy to eat the food you don't want."

"If only there were some way of giving it to them," we thought. "We would love to give them this awful fat on the meat." Betty and I both detested fat but father and mother both insisted we eat it. When they were not looking we quickly hid it under the table. We waited until mother wasn't home to dig a hole and bury it in the garden. It's a wonder that Father never discovered any of our secret caches of this disgusting fat.

A special treat was golden treacle on toast–something comforting that reminded mother of her childhood in England. She wanted to bring us up in the English way. Although she was a nurse, she still believed in some of the good old-fashioned remedies for 'curing what ails you'. Sniffing table salt dissolved in tap water was her remedy for post nasal drip and she firmly believed in lemon juice in warm water every morning to ward off colds. Now, people take vitamin C, instead.

Father was doing well and bought more land in nearby Coquitlam. We even had a cottage, on the hill on Buena Vista Road, overlooking the water in White Rock. We were always so excited when father would say, "Get your things together. We're going to the beach!" Then we would all pile excitedly into the car and head down the King George Highway, up and over the hill. All of a sudden, there before us, we could see the water of Semiamhoo Bay, glistening in the hot summer sun. White Rock in the 1920's was a typical seaside village with, what seemed to us, miles of sand, warm water and a long pier where we learned to swim. The Great Northern trains, on their way to Seattle and points south, delivered passengers to the beach daily. It was great fun to see the train pass through the little town. We would play all day with our pails and sand shovels, making castles, surrounding them with moats and watching, fascinated, as the water rushed in and filled our little trenches. When the tide came in, Auntie Theda would hold us by the straps on our bathing suits and pull us in over the deepest water. Tired, and quite likely sunburned, we would order fish and chips in cardboard cones, splashed with malt vinegar, tasty, salty and utterly satisfying. "Very English," mother would say.

Sometimes father took us all to English Bay or to Stanley Park in the big city of Vancouver. Father had the concession to remove the hornwort from Beaver Pond–a job for the whole family. Father and mother enjoyed the cricket matches while we children loved swimming at one of the park's beaches. It was a special treat in the summer, if we stayed late enough, to hear the famous nine o'clock gun, a cannon fired off on the dot of nine every night.

Even Jack was contented on those days and he did seem happier for a time. He earned pocket money delivering the local newspaper, *The British Columbian,* on his bike every afternoon. In those days before local radio and television, most families eagerly awaited the daily paper to read all the news that was 'fit to print'. And *The Columbian* did print everything from the daily news to accounts of tea parties and weddings. No event was too small to be reported, especially if it was a 'no news' day. Every father in New Westminster sat down in the living room after dinner to read the paper while the women of the house washed and dried the dishes. With the last chores of the day completed, the women could sit down with a cup of tea and read the small town gossip and, in summer, the children were free to play outside while it was still light.

Birthdays were special occasions. Once, we filled the living room with paper streamers and fresh flowers for Betty's birthday. Another time we went to Burr's, the stationery store owned by the parents of Raymond Burr of Perry Mason fame. There we learned to make crepe paper flowers and then decorated the living room with garlands of pastel, crepe paper blossoms. One year the whole class came for a party. And, there was always a birthday cake. Mother would wrap little treasures, trinkets or coins in waxed paper and bake them in the cake. You can bet every child ate her cake very carefully.

We were just like all the other families we knew around us. While we did have a car and everything we needed, Betty and I didn't have skates or bicycles but I don't think we felt deprived. We mostly made our own fun and we were happy. Betty and I played house and she always wanted to play school. Of course, she had to be the teacher. I never could see the point of pretending to be in school when you were lucky to be out of the real classroom, but I usually gave in to Betty. Most importantly, we always had good books in the house. Father, who loved reading, passed on a love of books to me that has stayed with me all my life. It was a long walk to the beautiful old Carnegie Library on Carnarvon Street but we often found ourselves under its lovely dome, hushed, not by the librarians, but by all the books surrounding us.

Betty and I looked forward eagerly every spring to the annual May Day celebration in Queen's Park. Some lucky little girl was chosen to be May Queen for the year and one girl from each elementary school became part of the 'Royal Party'. On the appointed day, if the day was fine the anvil salute sounded at the Armory. We then hurried down to watch the big May Day parade on Columbia Street. In the afternoon we donned our best dresses and all trouped off to Queen's Park to dance around the May poles. The past and present May Queens made speeches as did a venerable old man, J.J. Johnson, who had been a babe in his mother's arms at the very first May Day. In the evening, there was a ball at which the mayor of the day and various city dignitaries danced the lancers with the Royal Party. Mother and father loved this very English celebration.

Did mother and father regret leaving Invermere? If they did, we never heard them say so, but once we took a trip in our Model T up the Fraser Canyon past Chilliwack and on through Boston Bar to Seton Lake. Perhaps they were considering a move back to a smaller community. I wonder if Father was still chasing the pot of gold at the end of another rainbow.

Then came the lean years of the Great Depression and I remember my father, one day, announcing "The bottom dropped out of the market."

"Was anyone hurt?" I asked, thinking of the market where we sold the vegetables and berries we grew in our garden. It was 1929 and the stock market had crashed. People had no money for extras like fishponds and goldfish. Men often knocked on our kitchen door, asking for food in exchange for chopping kindling for the stove, or some other yard work. I'm sure my mother never turned them away, always giving them some job to do so they kept their self-respect. They were tough times for us all. But it was only the beginning of trouble for Betty and me.

First there was trouble between mother and father. Sometimes we would hear raised voices and angry words exchanged. Once I remember being shocked to see a shoe hurled through one of the windows. Betty and I tried to block our ears and pretend that we were a happy family. By this time we knew that mother was ill and in pain. She had breast cancer and had one breast removed. We thought she was better but the cancer returned and, one day, an ambulance arrived at our house and took her to the Royal Columbian Hospital. As soon as we saw her lying in the hospital bed we knew she could not recover. I remember hearing her say to father, bitterly, "Don't worry, you won't be long behind me." She even made plans for her funeral and told us what clothes we should wear to it.

"Mind you wear your dark dresses," she said. "No one will expect you girls to wear black. I know you will look out for each other and take care of your father."

I was twelve when she died. It was a cold, windy day in 1929, so bleak, sad, and snowing, the day of her funeral. Dressed as she instructed us, we stood at the graveside and said our tearful good-byes. It was up to Betty and me now, to do the cooking and cleaning as well as go to school. Worse troubles were as near as around the next corner.

Father was already suffering from rheumatoid arthritis and emphysema. Now I realize that handling the gypsum led to his lung problems.

Around the time our stepmother died, I began to fear him. He had always been stern with us but Jack was the only one of us to feel his wrath in a physical way. Now he began to come to my room at night and stand in my doorway. He was on crutches by this time. Typical of most girls in the 1920's I was sexually innocent but some inner voice warned me to fear him. Mother was no longer here to protect us. "Get out of here!" I screamed at him more than once. Fortunately, he always turned away.

And, before long, father also had cancer. He now stayed in bed the whole day. I lost my fear of him. When he could no longer hurt me, I tried to keep him company. We played cards and chess everyday when I returned from school. It was at this time that he told me the story of his boyhood. He was the only boy in a family of thirteen sisters. A handsome man, he was born in West Hartlepool and educated at a famous Masonic school. The curriculum must have included many subjects because he seemed to be good at so many things. We even had a table carved with flowers that he had never finished because he ran a chisel through one of the fingers on his left hand while making it. He told me he had nearly died of blood poisoning. Hurting his hand had also curtailed his ambition to be a violinist although he did play for a while with an orchestra in New Westminster.

Not long after he left school he decided to come to Canada. "There were no prospects for a lad like me in the old country," he told me. Like many new immigrants before the First World War, he tried farming on the prairies. He brought his mother out to keep house for him but she hated the cold winters. One morning he saw her weeping, the tears freezing on her cheeks.

"That was enough," he told me. "I took her back to

My grandfather, Erdmann Gottlieb Martin Sellentin.

My grandmother, Elizabeth Annie Hall.

England and returned to Canada with a new bride, your mother." What my mother thought of the prairies, I'll never really know, but soon after, in 1909, my parents left and settled in Invermere. My brother was born in 1913, and that was when my mother, homesick for her English home in Windsor, took her new baby back to her family.

Coming to Canada, my father was sure he had all the skills he needed to succeed and, in the good years in Invermere, he did prosper. He did well in New Westminster too, before the Depression. Now, he lay in bed most of the time. His hands, that had served him so well, were gnarled and painful, his breathing laboured. When he did get up, he hobbled through the house on crutches. He knew he was dying and said, to reassure himself as much as us, "You'll be all right." He knew he could do nothing more for us. He didn't want to leave us but it was too late for regrets.

I was thirteen when father died in January. He was just forty-nine. When the ambulance came to take him to the hospital, Betty went with him. He never came home again. His funeral was another very cold, bleak day and we forgot to close the door to the greenhouse. All our goldfish were frozen. We were all alone. I remember sitting on the stairs and wondering what we were going to do. Those stairs are still there. When I revisited our house and saw them again for the first time in seventy years, the memories came flooding back. I could see the two of us, Betty and I, knowing there was no one to turn to. Mother's friends, Auntie Theda and Auntie LaBelle had moved away. We had no idea where they were.

"Why don't we write to dad or mother's families in England?" I asked. "Remember how father told us his aunt came out to Invermere after our mother died?"

"How would we find them?" Betty answered. "One thing, for sure," I remember her saying, "We've got to stick together."

Remembering father's words, "You'll be all right," I knew that if we survived, it would be without Jack's aid. He had never been much help and was now gone most of the time, only coming home late at night. We learned later, when he started to sell our furniture and pictures, that he was drinking and gambling. Betty and I knew the best thing to do as far as Jack was concerned, was to stay out of his way. He was never home, anyway.

Although there were many people at father's funeral, hardly anyone seemed to realize that we were two young girls alone, with no money. I suppose everyone thought that Jack, who by now was a young man of 18, was taking care of us. I'm sure father expected that of him. We were all naïve.

Norman Lidster, a local lawyer, was father's executor. He told us that father's will stipulated that we could only receive the proceeds of his estate when we were twenty-one. Perhaps this was true, because Father may have intended to prevent Jack from selling our house. We did not ask to see the will because we trusted Mr. Lidster. I am convinced that our trust was misplaced. When Betty and I turned twenty-one, there was no money at all for us. No money from our house, the acreage in Coquitlam, or the beach cottage in White Rock. On the other hand, it was the Depression, and the properties weren't worth much.

We looked through all father's papers but there was nothing to tell us how to find our relatives far away in England. Both our parents seemed to have lost contact with our grandparents, aunts, and uncles. I've often wondered about that. Dad, with his thirteen sisters, especially. Didn't they wonder what had happened to us?

One lady, our neighbour Mrs. Butters, must have been aware that we needed help, but even she had no idea how bad things really were. Often all we had to eat was a slice of bread with a little mayonnaise on it. She sometimes invited us for a meal but not once did we let on that we had no money except what we could badger from Jack. Sometimes we did receive a hamper from one of the churches, so perhaps someone did suspect we were desperate. If asked, I don't know if we could have told anyone that we had no money. Like father, we were too proud to reveal that we were destitute. Also, Betty and I knew full well that we might be separated if anyone did discover our plight. Separated or sent to the Loyal Protestant Home, an orphanage very visible in New Westminster then. Everyone knew the 'orphanage kids'. It wasn't as if they were badly cared for but we thought we were too old to be treated like children.

Somehow, we got through the rest of that bleak winter and spring. In the summer, Betty and I earned a little money selling sweet peas door to door at five cents a bunch. We planted a vegetable garden just as dad had taught us and we had our own strawberries and raspberries. Jack was never home. It was no use asking him for money, anyway. He didn't care about us.

When summer ended we were forced to find a solution before another rainy, dark winter set in. At that time, the only high schools in the area were in New Westminster and many girls from the Fraser Valley and Coquitlam 'lived in' with local families. The girls attended school and helped out with cooking, cleaning and child care after school and on weekends. Betty went to live with a nice family, doing housework for them. They allowed her to continue school. I was not so lucky. The lawyer, Mr. Lidster, found me a job with his next door neighbour, Mrs. Mellers, who had pernicious anemia. For eight dollars a week, I would go in each morning, do her dishes and other housework and make her lunch. I was often so hungry that I would steal a piece of bread when I arrived. I can never cook liver without remembering how often I cooked it in those days for Mrs. Mellors. Doctors, even back then, knew that liver was a source of iron for anemic patients. If I was happy, I sang while I worked. Mrs. Mellors would shout, "Can't you sing anything but that awful *Fishies in the Ocean?*" But, it was the singing that kept my spirits up. I sang as I dreamt about getting married and having a home of my own and not having to worry about anything. Sometimes though, in my dreams, I saw myself a career woman like Auntie LaBelle.

Finally I had the good fortune to get a job with Captain and Mrs. D. D. Archibald. They had four boys and, for $8.00 a week including room and board I had to help with everything, cooking, cleaning, washing and ironing, polishing shoes. It was hard work but it also meant I could leave home and 'live in'. As far as I was concerned I was, like Betty, escaping and I couldn't have found a better employer than Mrs. Archibald. She was a lovely Scottish lady, very down to earth and practical. She taught me how to iron and what's more, she was an excellent cook and patiently taught me all she knew. I still have her recipe for scones and oatcakes. She also taught me to be a good manager. I had my own, very feminine bedroom with a little dressing table with a pink skirt and a mirror. No one in the house minded me singing! I was able to continue my education at night school. Later, when I had a home of my own and then ran my own motel in Kamloops, I was proud of my ability to manage a house and run a business. Mrs. Archibald set me on that path to success.

When I went back to our house to pick up the rest of my clothes a few days after going to work for the Archibald family, I saw that my brother had sold everything, even the toilet! I was right. I had escaped.

Chapter 2

Jack

It's strange, but I cannot remember meeting my first husband. I know Betty met her husband Gordon, at a dance, and perhaps that was where I first saw Jack Ogden. It might have been at the Scandinavian dance hall on Hastings Street in Vancouver, because even in those days I loved to dance. Perhaps I met him at the movies. Betty and I went as often as we could to the Columbia or Edison theatres in New Westminster or we took the interurban tramline into Vancouver to go dancing. In those days you could see a double feature, two movies for the price of one. We never tired of our favourite Hollywood stars like Jean Harlow or Bette Davis. We'd go home and try to do our hair like they did and imagine ourselves living like they did. I never wanted to see gory movies though. If Betty did persuade me to see a horror show, at the frightening scenes, I would put my head down and say, "Tell me when it's over!"

Jack was handsome and, I thought, sophisticated. He had a bold look about him that made him seem fearless and he was fun in a wild sort of way. He was over ten years older than I was and made me feel protected. And I suppose I was impatient and eager to escape again. As grateful as I was to Mrs. Archibald, I couldn't see much of a future for myself doing housework in New Westminster. Perhaps too, I envied Betty, who by the time I met Jack, had married Gordon and moved into a nice little home right away. Betty, though, had her doubts. "He's too old for you, Margaret," she warned. "Don't be in so much of a hurry to settle down."

I married Jack a year later. I was just seventeen. Mrs. Archibald also pointed out that I was too young to get married. "Marry in haste, repent in leisure," she reminded me. "Why don't you just wait a year or so, dear?" she continued. However, once she saw how determined I was, she helped me choose my white wedding dress and long veil.

"I hope, for your sake, it works out," she said. I know I was like a daughter to her and she wanted me to have the best marriage with a good husband. More than anything though, I wanted a home, a place of my own. For the time being, thinking I was in love, I put the idea of being a businesswoman out of my mind.

Soon after the wedding, I became very sick with a high temperature and terrible stomach pains. I soon found myself back at the Royal Columbian Hospital. Out came my appendix. As I lay in bed recovering, I had plenty of time to think about the mess I was in. I dreaded going back home and even dreaded Jack's visits to the hospital.

After my operation, Jack, who worked for the CNR,

arrived at the hospital with the news that he had been transferred to Kamloops. In the hospital, I met a lovely nurse, Jean Glenville. When I told her I was moving to Kamloops, she told me that her sister, Laura McPherson, who was also a nurse, lived there. Thanks to Jean, I met Laura and we soon became lifelong friends. I'm sure Jean suspected I needed a friend.

The marriage was not a success. In fact, I knew it was a mistake from the first night. Looking out the stateroom window on the ship to Victoria, on our wedding night, I thought, "What have I got myself into?" At seventeen, I was far too young. Jack was thirteen years older. It was my first serious relationship. Later he told me, "People said I robbed the cradle." Perhaps I was looking for a father. Jack was not fit to be a husband or a father.

I was innocent and Jack was sexually demanding. I dreaded hearing his footsteps when he came home at the end of his shift at the railway yards. He wanted sex on demand and he was no lover. Sometimes he wouldn't even wait until after he had bathed and cleaned himself up from his greasy black day's work as a mechanic. As long as I met his needs, he was satisfied. Often, at night, I would lie awake long after he was asleep, unfulfilled, unsatisfied. There were no sex therapists in those days and anyway, I would have died rather than tell anybody the intimate details of our marriage. I would not even tell Betty or my closest friends how awful it was. It wasn't until much later I learned that sex with someone you love is a joyful part of marriage.

Inside the cover of my *Blue Ribbon Cookbook*, its pages worn from so much use, is the address of our first home, 607 5th Avenue in New Westminster. Even if sex was unpleasant I wanted to be a good homemaker, to make Jack proud of me and to make our home a cozy retreat. At first, I thought I could change our relationship if only Jack could see how much I tried to please him. I used all the valuable homemaking skills Mrs. Archibald taught me. I enjoyed making all our curtains and pillows, tending the little garden and making a good dinner for him when he came home from work. I was sure I could win him over.

It was useless. Anything could set him off. He was jealous and never wanted me to be out of the house. He didn't like Betty or my new girl friends, either. Perhaps he imagined I was telling them about him. When he was full of rage he would yell at me and throw things, whatever was at hand, dishes of course, but even a stick of wood. I was happiest when he was on shift work, sleeping in the daytime, gone at night. Then, if I saved a little cash from the housekeeping money Jack grudgingly gave me, I could escape to make-believe land at the movies and Jack was none the wiser.

Jack was offered a foreman's position and wouldn't take it. I couldn't understand his lack of ambition. It would have meant more money for us, a better job and a chance for further promotions in the company for him. To give him credit, he was always a hard worker. He just didn't want the responsibility of supervising other men.

I, on the other had, could hear my father saying, "Aim high and you will always land someplace on the horizon!" Perhaps what he had said to us before he died, "You'll be all right," echoed in my mind as well. I would be all right! But I could see that if we were going to get anywhere, it would be up to me.

Arriving in Kamloops, we lived in two rooms in a boarding house where we did our own cooking. Betty, by this time, had two children and every time I saw her babies, Carole and Keath, I longed for a child of my own. It didn't happen. Remembering Auntie Labelle's example, I found two part time jobs; one in Beaton's dress shop and the second, in Webber's jewelry shop. I loved working and earning my own money. It meant I was not so dependent on Jack and didn't have to ask him for housekeeping money.

I developed a clothes sense at the dress shop. It was the first time I had the opportunity to see fashionable and well made clothes. I learned about good clothes, and how to co-ordinate outfits stylishly. I sometimes modeled the clothes as well and could buy things at a discount. Prairie people, Jim and Vera Beaton who had settled in Kamloops, owned the shop. They told me, "Our dresses sell themselves with you as our model." At the dress shop I also met many people who were helpful to me later when I went into business for myself.

Working in the jewelry store, I learned about gemstones and how to check watches for the engineers on the railroads. We had a book in which we recorded officially that we had checked a watch. Those trains were expected to run on time! I can still see the owner, Mr. Webber, a fussy little man, looking intently through his eyepiece at one of the beautiful gemstones in his shop.

Both Betty and I were clothes conscious ever since the time we used to hide them in the trunk in our fort in the bush. We were attractive and knew we looked good. What we didn't know was that our good looks could get us into trouble. I remember that some time after father, died Betty and I took the interurban tram into Vancouver for a newspaper photography shoot that we saw announced in the paper. We had both been in plays by then and maybe we hoped we'd be discovered by Hollywood. People called us the 'beautiful sisters'. The two of us laughed but felt a little guilty at the same time. We knew, that if father had been alive, he would never have allowed us to do this. He was so strict with us that he even insisted that we wear our hair long, perhaps reminding him of our mother's lovely hair. I defied him by cutting my hair in the last few months of his life. He was so angry he refused to have me in his room, saying, "Don't come in here". Eventually he relented.

Betty and I, along with two other Vancouver 'glamour girls', were featured in an article in *The Province*. There we were, Betty and I, pictured as "The flowers of Western Canadian girlhood…faces freshly scrubbed and free of makeup". According to the reporter, Betty had ambitions to be a business-woman and I was longing for a nest with a family. Funny how it turned out for us, exactly the opposite! The photographer said, "You should go to Hollywood," and offered to take us to California. We were not the little innocents he thought we were. Even in quiet little New Westminster we heard of 'casting couch' stories. After the other girls who showed up for the shoot left, he took us both aside and suggested taking one or two special pictures. We could make a little more money if we allowed him to take nude pictures of us.

"What kind of pictures?" I asked.

He explained the photographs would be tastefully done. We could make twenty dollars more if we agreed.

"Why not?" I said to Betty.

"What if someone finds out?" she asked.

"Don't be silly," I remember saying. "No one will find out if you don't tell and you can bet I won't."

We knew better than to accept his offer of a free trip to California, but we needed the money he was offering us. Twenty dollars seemed like a fortune to us, and posing for the pictures seemed harmless. There was no one at home to tell us not to do it, although we knew neither of our parents would ever have allowed it.

So, we did it. He took us to a secluded beach, away from curious eyes. We were minors and, although we didn't know it at the time, he could have been charged with corrupting us.

The pictures were beautiful. We were proud of ourselves, but I understood right away that no one we knew should ever see them. We had trouble collecting our money from the photographer, too. Maybe he thought he could blackmail us by refusing to pay for the pictures he used in the paper, threatening to show the secret ones. When we phoned his home to demand our money, his wife answered. She said she didn't know anything about it our pay. Did she know about the special pictures? We finally got our money when Gordon, Betty's fiancé, phoned and demanded our money.

"Promise me you'll never tell anyone about them," Betty begged. I assured her that our secret was safe with me. We both had second thoughts but it was too late for regrets, now.

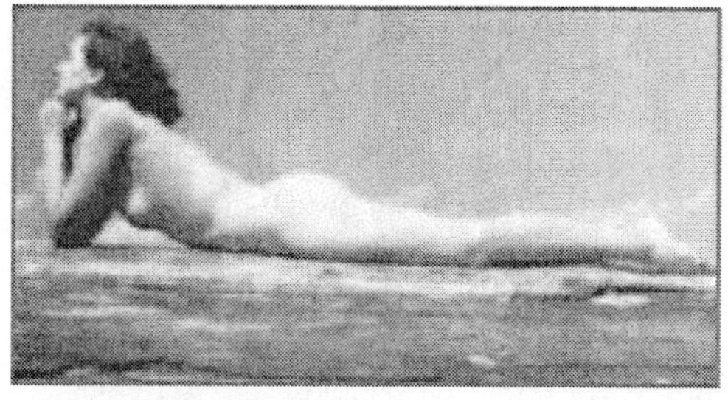

Me! About Sweet 16
Opposite page: Vancouver Girls Have Natural Glamor

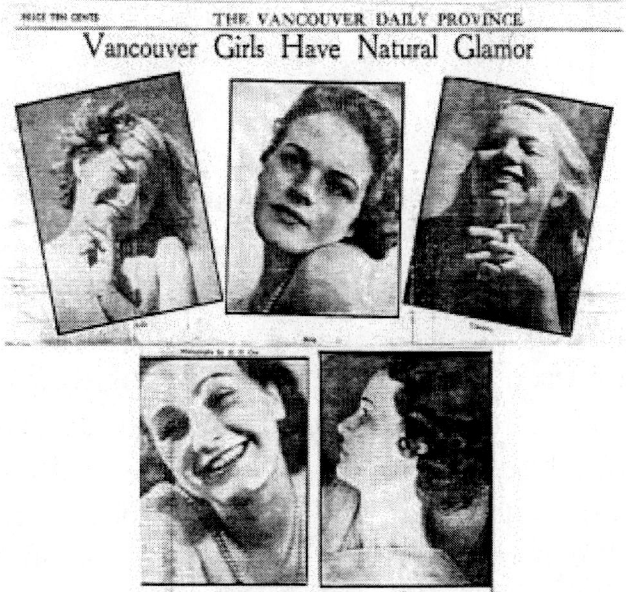

THE VANCOUVER DAILY PROVINCE

Vancouver Girls Have Natural Glamor

INTRODUCING Vancouver girls!

Other cities, other countries may have their glamour girls, their sport girls, their mystery or their pretty girls, but Vancouver has—Vancouver girls.

Healthy, wholesome and radiant with life, they need no sympathetic buildup from shaded lights, from rows of glass-topped powder jars before they face the camera.

They got none. Faces freshly scrubbed and shinning, eyes wide and smiles natural, they were photographed as they appear here.

Now they symbolize the flower of western Canadian girlhood and young womanhood.

Betty is not yet out of her teens. She keeps house for an invalid parent, and has the faint reserve of a gentle but convincing dignity. She enjoys music and good books, is fond of the great outdoors. Her teeth are even and white and her petal-smooth skin photographs to perfection without the slightest aid from makeup.

Her naturally wavy chestnut hair is an aura of changing light about her perfectly moulded features, which photograph very well from any angle. There is a faint air of mystery about her.

Margaret loves life, music and dancing, is not over-indulgent in strenuous sports, but enjoys being out-of-doors. She might be a successful artist's model wither five feet four of lissom grace, but her ambition is to make her own home. She has even, clear-cut features and auburn hair which falls to her shoulders in thick, loose waves. Her long, sweeping eyelashes shadow large, expansive hazel eyes. She is wholly feminine.

Reprinted courtesy of Pacific Press.

Both Betty and I chose traditional paths for women of our day. We married and settled down as homemakers. Betty and Gordon really did have a storybook marriage, settling in a storybook cottage in New Westminster. I envied them because I knew by now that I would never have that kind of marriage with Jack.

As much as possible, I tried to hide my unhappiness, and, when I was twenty-one, I had a phone call from a gentleman from Metropolitan Life telling me my father had taken out a small life insurance policy. Betty and I each received $500. It was a respectable legacy when a pound of butter cost a good deal less than a dollar and with four dollars you could easily buy a good pair of shoes. With what I saved from my two jobs and the $500, Jack and I were just able to put a down payment on our own small house. We paid $2,400. The year was 1939. Canada would soon be at war.

It was fun decorating our first home on Pleasant Street. I made curtains from flour sacks with bands of red tape. I found that with just a little money and a lot of imagination you could make a house attractive. We built a suite in the basement and rented it to a new friend, Uncle Ben, as we called him.

Uncle Ben was the master mechanic for the western division of the CNR. It seems he knew Father from away back and he was very kind to me and, later, to Betty. He was a short, dapper little man. He always wore spats and a felt Homberg. For special occasions, he was never

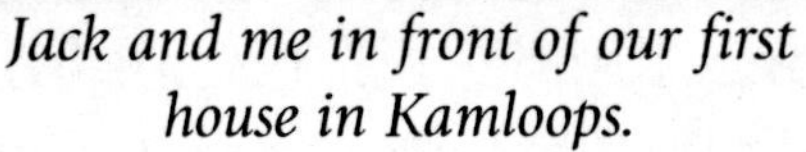

Jack and me in front of our first house in Kamloops.

Uncle Ben.

without his white silk scarf. He was as fussy as heck, couldn't stand a blade of grass out of place and, according to Jack, was far too nice. He had firm ideas about women, too. Only bad girls smoked, drank or gambled. I should have known that Jack was jealous of Uncle Ben but there was never anything between us. He was unhappily married to Catholic woman who refused to divorce him. He had a son and daughter of his own, but his wife would never allow him to see them. When we first knew him, as strange as it seems now, he was living in a boxcar. He was always grateful that we made a home for him with us. To Uncle Ben, I was like a daughter. Just the same, though, I was aware of the gossip about us. My real friends knew the truth about my relationship with Uncle Ben, but not about my secret life with Jack.

Around this time Betty, Jack and I returned to visit our old home in Invermere. All our lives had changed so much in the intervening years. It was hard to believe so much had happened to all of us since Father built the little homestead in the wilderness.

Our old home in 1939.

The old home.

Soon our Canada was at war. It seemed as if it would never end and it made us very careful. Remembering everything father had taught me in New Westminster, I planted a garden. We grew petunias and all our own vegetables, tomatoes, potatoes, lettuce, green onions, radishes, carrots and green beans. Kamloops was the best place to grow tomatoes and those sun-ripened ones were delicious. We even had raspberry canes and I recall being so proud of all the jars of vegetables, fruit, pickles and jams I put up. It was the thing to do and I did it!

I also joined the Kinettes during the war. As well as making friends with other women, we rolled a lot of bandages and knitted socks for the war effort.

In Kamloops, I began my life-long joy in the game of golf. I loved it right from the start. Some of the boys from the CNR and CPR cleared the sagebrush and made a nine-hole course above the town. It was hard work. The greens were anything but green. In fact, they were sand. We had a stick with a piece of canvas that we dragged across the sand to make it smooth. We used tomato cans for the holes and teed off from rubber mats.

It's great to be out in the fresh air knowing that a good game is all up to you. You have to keep your mind on what you are doing and you forget everything else. Unlike at school, I never had any trouble concentrating at work or on the golf course.

I was trying to ignore the bad times with Jack. When he was happy, he whistled. When he was angry, what started with finger tapping displeasure became uglier physical and mental abuse. To outsiders, his charm and good looks hid a meaner side.

The good thing about Jack working on the railroad was that, as his wife, I had a pass and could travel free. Betty was still living in New Westminster and I often went down to visit with her. Perhaps, because she disliked Jack, she never invited the two of us down for Christmas with her family. Jack would taunt me, saying, "See, even your sister doesn't want you!" He called me careless and blamed me for losing my wedding and engagement rings. Later I discovered he had hidden them in my face powder. Once, right after we planted new grass, he was angry about something and pulled out the stakes from around the new lawn hurling them at me. Of course, Jack was careful never to let anyone else see this other side of him. If Uncle Ben was in the house, he kept his temper, sometimes just barely. To our friends, we seemed like the perfect couple. I suppose my new friends Laura and Connie suspected my unhappiness, but I thought there was no way out of this marriage. I still didn't dare tell anyone what was happening at home, away from view, behind closed doors. I thought it was up to me to make the marriage work. If Jack was angry it must be my fault. I tried not to let him see how miserable I really was because if I had, it would only have made him angrier. Often I thought about my father and stepmother. Their marriage had not been a happy one either. And yet, Betty and Gord were a happy couple and I also remembered Captain and Mrs. Archibald. Theirs was a marriage of deep contentment and mutual respect.

Jack's father was shop foreman at the Jasper roundhouse so, when we had some free time, we would go up there to play on the wonderful golf course. I met the head pro and played golf with his assistant. Mrs. Brinkworth, the head pro's wife, taught me invaluable golf course etiquette; how and where to stand, how to mark a ball, and, above all, to be quiet and not disturb another golfer's concentration on the game. I've played golf all over the world. Thanks to Mrs. Brinkworth, nobody ever called me a 'duffer'. Jack enjoyed golf, too, and would never show his true colours on the greens. I was safe there from his temper.

Around this time, Jack and I took a trip down to the States, to the Columbia River with Uncle Ben. This trip gave me the idea to start a motor court. It was an idea that wouldn't go away. But first, we decided to build a cabin at Paul Lake.

We were bowling one Sunday afternoon when Chuck Turnbull joined us. He was in Kamloops, working for the government, building housing for soldiers. He had caught some fish that day so we invited him up to the house where I cooked his catch for dinner. We became good friends with Chuck and his wife and family when they joined him eventually. We told Chuck that we wanted to build a place at Paul Lake. I had such happy memories of the fun at the cottage on the beach at White Rock. I wanted to build a cabin at Paul Lake, make it a place to invite our friends and to enjoy cottage life again. Maybe it would even help to make things better between Jack and I.

The Indians owned the land around Paul Lake and we learned that it wouldn't cost much to take a 99-year lease on a lot there. We found our property right on the water opposite a big bluff. Chuck drew the plans for us. I put down my golf clubs and took up my hammer. It was fun building Fir Croft. For one thing, when Jack and I worked side by side, things were better between us. I think Jack was surprised when he discovered, that thanks to my father's training, I could hammer and saw with the best of the boys.

The cottage had a large living room, two small bedrooms and a kitchen and bathroom with a sink but no toilet. There was an outhouse out back. Uncle Ben, who sure could use a hammer, helped us and we built a deck. I made curtains and matching covers for the seats under the corner windows. We had water pumped up from the lake and a generator for lights. Everyone loved to come up to the cabin. They came for the good fishing, good swimming in warm water and good times. They all brought something to contribute to our picnics. Chuck, his wife Edie and their two children, Doreen and Kenneth, Betty, Gordon and their children, everyone loved it.

Renting the cottage also gave me some extra money. I would give people the key and a map and they were off for a few days at the lake. Sometimes, even now, more than fifty years later, I take out the guest book and read the enthusiastic comments friends wrote. And I learned a life-lesson that when you share your good fortune you never have regrets. There was never any damage, and friends always left it clean and tidy. I was still holding on to the motor court idea, though. We decided to build in 1945.

Above: Betty and me at Kamloops
Left: Me
Right: Jack and me

Betty and her husband Gordon and Jack.

Cottage at Paul Lake .

Edith Turnbull.

Fish at Paul Lake.

Kenny and Chuck Turnbull with Tuffy.

Carol and me at Paul Lake.

Me on Paul Lake.

Jack and Carol.

Sister Betty at Paul Lake.

Doreen, Tuffy and Carol.

Chapter 3

Taking Care of Business—The Mayfair Motor Court

The cottage finished, we sold our first home for nine thousand dollars and bought a few acres on veteran-held land out at Valleyview. I drew up the plans, which the District had to approve. I don't know how many women the permit people had dealt with but they were never patronizing and, in fact, went out of their way to help us. We had to put in a road and pipe in water. There was so much to do. It was a busy time but fun seeing the work progress. Jack, of course, was still working on the railway, so I did most of the planning, contracting and legwork.

Once we completed the house, we built an office with a small store and a storage room with a washing machine. Finally, we added a building with three suites, all with cooking facilities. We opened the Mayfair Motor Court in 1946.

Every day I got up at six. Once again, if I wasn't wielding a hammer, painting or building a rockery in the garden, I was at my sewing machine. I made all the drapes and bedspreads myself and bought towels and linens in pretty pastel colours co-ordinated with the pink and rose décor. I always put fresh flowers from my own garden in all the suites, and books as well.

When we opened, my first customer was a young Japanese man. It felt strange because we had been at war with the Japanese, and the government relocated so many Japanese Canadians during the war–a sad story. He left a thank you note on his pillow with a dollar bill. I still have it. There's no such thing as an eight-hour day in the motel business or any other business you own and operate yourself. As soon as I heard guests go off in their cars, I would be up, cleaning the suites, making the beds and doing the laundry. As soon as people smelled the coffee they knew the day had started for me.

There was no dryer so I had to hang all the sheets and towels on a line. Nothing beats that fresh clean smell of sheets and towels dried outside.

Sweet smelling sheets were just one of the touches I prided myself on providing. I realized that running a motor court was just housekeeping on a large scale and I tried to keep the units the way I kept my own home. Sure I got tired, sometimes. In the tourist business, you wear a smile no matter how tired you are. I was used to 'keeping a smile on my face' living with Jack. Nothing made him madder than if I looked less than ecstatic to see him. One thing was very different now, though. Unlike Jack, the customers were always very appreciative. We were busy all year long with sales and business people, and tourists who kept coming back to our place, time after time.

Printed in the Vancouver paper reprinted courtesy of Pacific Press.

Here for the Auto Courts and Resorts Association convention in Hotel Vancouver, Mrs. Ogden thinks tourists are wonderful, Kamloops is wonderful, her fellow owners are wonderful, and especially, her own motor court at Kamloops is wonderful.

This despite the fact that her 12-hour day covers every kind of chore, from registering guests, supervising cleaning of the units, clerking in the small store attached, to attending to buying of supplies and keeping of accounts.

HELPED BUILD IT

She takes a motherly pride in the court, since a lot of it was built with her own two hands.

"I put down my golf clubs and took up a hammer," she recalled, "and I haven't had a minute to play golf since."

Strictly a babe-in-the-woods when it came to business, Mrs. Ogden learned early in her tourist court days to rely on other people.

"What I know, I'll do," she said, "but what I don't know, I'll ask."

DID ALL SEWING

She did know how to sew before she went into the business, so all the modern drapes and bedspreads in the twelve units are products of her dewing machine.

"And in my spare time now, I get out and push rocks around in the garden," she said.

There's little spare time, however, since the court is a year round proposition, and "there's always something going on in Kamloops to draw visitors."

KEEP SMILING

"Sure I get tired sometimes," the vivacious young woman admitted, "but in this business you have to wear a smile no matter how tired you get."

Mrs. Ogden prides herself on the appearance of her court and on the type of customers she attracts.

"It's just housekeeping on a large scale," she said, "and I try to keep the units the way I would my own home. And if the place is nice the customers will treat it well."

In proof of this, she reported that her only losses form the cabins are "the odd towel." "And that's rare," she said.

Mayfair Motor Court, Kamloops, B.C.

Sometimes my customers felt so much at home that they even pitched in and helped with the chores. One lady said she just loved getting right in the garden, pulling up weeds, pruning and tidying up. No wonder the Mayfair always looked so good!

Having the store was fun, too. We carried the basics–milk, bacon, eggs, some canned goods and we had a freezer for ice cream.

The motel business was proving lucrative. I can't believe now that we charged only $10.00 a night. Salesmen paid $5.00 and we gave people staying more that one night a discount. They paid $4.50! And we still made money.

Things were no better with Jack, though. He was jealous of the many salesmen who stayed with us. One day, in a fit of jealous rage, he cornered me in the laundry room. He had a butcher knife in his hand and there was no way I could get away from him. I knew, by now, that he would not hesitate to harm me. Fortunately, just as he was about to strike me, the bell rang in my office.

"You'd better go," he muttered. The customer who rang that bell would never know how thankful I was that he had interrupted Jack and rescued me from his attempt to hurt me, once again.

Another time, I was in Vancouver to do some shopping and lost my wallet. Not only was I without money, but my CNR pass was also gone. I knew Jack would be furious with me. I could hear him jeering, "You're so careless, Margaret–worse than a child. You'll just have to stay at home now, won't you?"

I was visiting with friends and, when they saw how upset I was, they called Uncle Ben and asked him to send another pass without letting Jack know about my wallet.

I borrowed money to build three more suites at a time. The bank was good about lending the money for lumber or an electric bill, but I never borrowed more than five hundred dollars at a time. When we had six suites I hired Jim Narroway, an accountant. All I had to do was keep all my sales slips and, of course, the guest register. Everybody paid cash in those days, before credit cards. Jim charged only fifteen dollars a month. I think he liked the drive out to the motor court and my office. It was then that I adopted my life-long habit of keeping good books and records. Uncle Ben had suite #4 and helped with the gardening when he wasn't travelling on the railroad.

I had my cabin at the lake, a new home and my business. My marriage, though, was over. Jack was becoming meaner. He had a truck and, although I was a good driver, he would never let me use it. "You think you're smart because you own a motel," he said. I thought, "Maybe you wish you had the same ambition." I hated him but most of the time I was so busy working, I tried not to think about the trouble between us.

By now, I had met the rest of Jack's family. In today's terminology, dysfunctional does not begin to describe them. His mother was a mean spirited, bitter woman who took delight in peering around the lace curtains in her living room windows, trying to see what her neighbours were up to, hoping to catch them out. After forty years, Jack's father eventually divorced this unhappy woman.

However, I was very fond of Jack's sister, Vimy, who was named for the famous battle her father fought and survived in the First World War. She was the only one of Jack's family to make me feel welcome. She was a lively girl who loved to dance and taught dancing to others. I loved to dance, too and we had so much fun learning the latest steps together.

While we were living in Kamloops, Vimy contracted TB and stayed with me before she went to the TB sanitarium at Tranquille. Our doctor warned me that Jack and I might easily come down with TB, too, so I reluctantly took her to King Edward Sanitarium. TB was a common illness at that time and we knew that, more often than not, its outcome was death. Before antibiotics, treatment consisted mostly of complete bed rest in wards where the windows were always open, no matter what the weather.

I took the bus regularly to visit Vimy while she was in the 'San', taking her chocolates, and fresh strawberries and raspberries from our garden. She was brave but anyone could see she was not getting better. She was so thin and her face had a feverish flush to it. She died at her parents' home in Jasper. It was heartbreaking, especially so, because she was so young and was the one person in her family with a zest for life.

I was busier than ever and meeting many nice folks who stayed at the motor court. Like every motel owner, though, I had my share of strange guests. Once a man and woman had a fight in their suite. After they left, I discovered tomato juice was their weapon of choice. It was all over the walls.

I'm pretty certain that I was not the only motor court owner called as a witness in a divorce case. It happened that a certain couple stayed in one of the suites on afternoons only. Later I was summoned to Penticton to testify in a divorce case in which the woman was involved. After everyone else had testified but before I could take my place on the stand, the judge cut the case off, saying to me, "Why gild the lily?" I was relieved. I would have been required to produce the guest register as evidence.

I did have one very famous customer, Mrs. Dodge of the Dodge Motor Company. Late one night Mrs. Dodge arrived in a limousine driven by her chauffeur. She was quite elderly and later I learned that she loved to fish. She gave her driver the night off and came to my door to ask me to open a can of beans. I went back to her suite and ended up making her dinner. She was a real darling, not pretentious at all. At the time,

I had no idea who she was. I was sad when I read of her death many years later.

Another of my interesting customers was the owner of the Sweet Sixteen Shops, a chain of women's clothing stores in B.C. He always stayed a week or more. He suffered from asthma and loved to sit in our garden. He couldn't read, so I often sat with him and read to him. A Jewish gentleman, he was very kind. I would always find a gift, a nice skirt and a blouse or sweater on the bed after he left. Other customers sent Christmas greetings every year.

Most travellers are honest. Aside from the odd towel, the only item ever stolen from me by a customer was a Hudson's Bay blanket. The police brought it back to me from the border crossing. I can't imagine the police concerning themselves with something so small in these days of weapons, terrorism and drug traffic.

I did lose my mother's gold bracelet and her opal and pearl brooch, though. I always thought they were stolen by a young girl I hired to help me clean the units but of course, I could never prove anything. She left soon after I asked her if she had seen them in my suite. If only she knew how precious these pieces were to me, not in monetary value but as the only mementos I had of my mother.

Suddenly Jack was gone. The railway transferred him to Prince Rupert. E. Davey Fulton, who later became a

Conservative cabinet minister in the federal government, arranged a legal separation. I confided in him, telling him about Jack's abusiveness and he had been advising me to do this for some time. We made the motor court into Mayfair Court Limited and had it appraised. Uncle Ben had 52% of the shares and I had 24%. I borrowed money from the bank to buy Jack's 24%. In fairness, he had worked hard to help us build the business and I wanted to do the right thing by giving him his share.

Just a few days before Jack left, I came home one day to find him throwing things into a fire in our back yard. When I saw what he was burning, I became stone cold. There was such bitter hatred and anger on his face as he stoked the fire with my wedding dress and veil, letters and all of our wedding pictures. I was thankful that he had not found the pictures taken by Mr. Cox. If in his rage, had he found them, he surely would have killed me. I couldn't wait for him to be gone, out of my life forever. I was so thankful.

We soon had twelve suites. We had a good, quiet location with clean, beautifully appointed and unique units. We were even highly recommended by Duncan Hines, and you couldn't pay your way into that guidebook. Dunn and Bradstreet also listed us. The owner of the New York Rangers farm team arranged for some of the hockey players to stay at the motel for the winter, our slow season. Everyone in town came out for the great Canadian national sport on Saturday nights in our small town. Then, the builders of the Trans Mountain

Pipeline billeted their men and even some of their wives with us. It meant that we were almost full up most of the year. We were doing well.

We also had a famous pet. Recently I read that the prestigious Vancouver Harbourside Hotel had a dog in residence. Guests enjoyed playing with the little pup in the lobby and could take him for a walk. The little fellow could even spend the night with a guest, no doubt sleeping right on the bed if he could get away with it. He was a big hit with everyone, kids and adults alike. We had Fritzi, the Mayfair Motel pet, back in the early 1950's. In fact, the local newspaper featured our dachshund in a newspaper article about our place. Fritzi had a friendly welcome for everyone and was not reluctant at all about paying visits to the guests in their units. Returning guests always looked for him first.

I often observed that even very lonely people could reach out to a little dog or cat. Pets ask no questions and love unconditionally. Sometimes when things were really bad between Jack and I, I would sit with Fritzi or take him for a walk, away from all the trouble.

With Jack gone and the business expanding I soon had more work than I could handle. I needed at least another pair of hands and a 36-hour day. Running a motor court is hard physical labour, cleaning the units, doing the laundry daily, keeping the garden looking attractive, and doing painting and repairs, not to mention shovelling snow in winter. I also had to make sure I kept

★★★★

The Mayfair Motor Court

IS SET OFF THE HIGHWAY FOR A GOOD NIGHT'S REST...JUST A 5—MINUTE DRIVE EAST OF KAMLOOPS ALONG THE TRANS-CANADA HIGHWAY.

Oil Heating – Bath and Showers
Spring-Filled Mattresses
Complete Home Units with Modern Kitchens
And Facilities.

KAMLOOPS' MOST EXCLUSIVE MOTOR COURT

RECOMMENDED BY DUNCAN HINES
AAA FOUR-STAR RATING

•

Mrs. Margaret Ogden
OWNER AND MANAGERESS

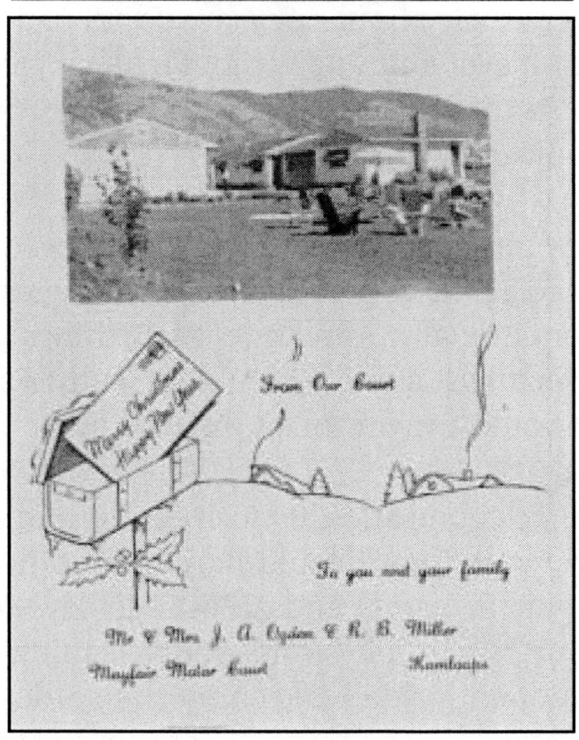

First Advertisement for the Mayfair Motor Court, 1947.

good books. Dorothy Harrop and Janet Fraser, two local women, were glad to come to work for me and proved invaluable. Dorothy's husband returned from the First World War a victim of poison gas; Janet's husband was the local veterinarian. Janet had a refreshing sense of humour and seemed to have a new joke to tell us every day. She had a phone but Dorothy didn't. Fortunately, Dorothy could see the motor court from her house so when I needed her, I would hang a red sweater on the door. When she saw that signal she would hurry on over to help. Dorothy's children were all grown up and away from home except for her young son, Les. He often stopped by on his way home from school to see if he could help. In return for running errands and doing little jobs for me, I would give him an ice cream cone or a chocolate bar. He was a lively, bright boy, and since I had no children of my own, I enjoyed his company.

At this time, a new highway closer to the Thompson River was under construction and some of the men would take Les with them in their trucks. One spring day I will never forget. The police drove up with the news that there had been an accident. Les was dead. He was in the cab of one of the trucks with a water tank they used to spray the road to settle the dust. The tank broke loose and crushed both Les and the driver. I went with the police to tell Dorothy. My heart broke for her as I held her in my arms, trying to comfort her but knowing no comfort was possible. Les was her baby. She never really got over his death but she thanked me for giving her work at the court. It gave her something to do, she said, and she stayed with me until I sold the business. I taught her to do needlework and when she wasn't working at the motor court or looking after her husband, she filled her hours with needlepoint. Nothing ever was the same for her again.

The new highway posed another problem for me. The old highway passed right in front of the motor court. The new one did not. I didn't own the land in front of the court so I couldn't put an access road to the new highway. Then another wonderful friend, Earl Peters, bought me the land as a birthday gift, so I could put a new road in. Good friends, Jim Wallace and his wife, also installed a bright neon sign. We still had our quiet location away from the noise of the busy highway but people could find us easily. These friends also sent me a lot of business.

Earl Peters on dock at Paul Lake.

Earl wanted me to take a trip to California. I felt I couldn't leave, and knew people would talk if I went alone with him, but Dorothy and Janet insisted on me going. They could look after the court. Even Uncle Ben thought I should get away. I was president of the Motel Owners Association of B.C. by this time and a Vancouver Sun reporter, Thelma Root, interviewed me during our annual general meeting. The headline ran "Babe in the Woods Does Okay with Auto Court." I didn't mind being called a 'babe'. I had money for the first time and could afford to dress the part. When I went down to Vancouver, I could buy my clothes in the exclusive Mirror Room of the Hudson's Bay and at Madame Rungés in the smart South Granville shopping district. I did admit to the reporter that I had little spare time. The truth was I had none. I was working 12 hours a day, seven days a week. I also said that I knew when to get help. That was true. I did what I could do best and found excellent people for the other jobs. Nevertheless, I still had all the responsibility and the others depended on me. I was proud of the Mayfair but I was tired. I don't think I realized, either, what a strain I had been under living with Jack. I decided to take a holiday.

'Babe-in-Woods' Does Okay With Auto Court

Reprinted courtesy of Pacific Press.

What a great trip we had down through Oregon into California. I always enjoyed the opportunity to compare my motor court with others in different places and I was interested to compare rates and come back with new ideas for better service. I wanted to be right up to date with trends in the business, as well. Being a customer for a change often gave me a whole new perspective on the motel business.

We stayed in Palm Desert for awhile to play golf. It was very warm there, but living in Kamloops, I was used to the heat. We went over to San Diego, saw their wonderful zoo, then headed north on the coast highway.

Earl was good company. He served with the Royal Flying Corps in World War I and later was George VI's chauffeur while he was the Duke of York. Earl could be very entertaining with his 'upstairs downstairs' version of the goings on at house parties at some of the great homes of England.

It was good to return home, though. I could see that Dorothy and Janet had done a fine job in my absence. But, good things never last. Earl had a stroke at his son's place and died soon after. I had lost a wonderful friend. He was a Shriner, a very good and kind man. I was happy that we had made that last trip together. It was the fall of 1952.

Life went on and the business prospered. Sometimes I would stand in the doorway of the office and wonder at the distance I had travelled since Betty and I sat on the front steps after our parents died. I was my own boss, I had good friends and I loved my life in Kamloops. After my trip south with Earl, I decided to take the time to play golf again. Getting away made me aware that I was dangerously close to what today we call 'burn out'. There had been so many changes in my life that, even though I was doing well, I had been under stress for many years. Living under the same roof as Jack had taken its toll.

Since then, I have always made time for my friends, my garden, my needlework and my painting. Although I don't play much golf these days, I've taken up lawn bowling because exercise is important, too.

Soon after Earl died, I met a nice chap, who stayed at the court when he came up from Medford, Oregon. Joe owned a lumber business. He was just a friend. I was not interested in marrying again. Those difficult years with Jack were behind me and I had no intention of getting entangled in another abusive relationship.

Chapter 4
My Darling Ted

My father always subscribed to *The National Geographic.* I kept up the tradition and never failed to turn to the last page to see the blue Cadillac featured there. I used to say to myself "Someday, girl, I'll see you behind the wheel of that car!" Now all my hard work was making my dream come true. I saved enough money to buy a new car and the dealers in Kamloops said it would be cheaper to pick it up in Windsor, Ontario. I decided to fly back east. Uncle Ben, at sixty-eight, decided to retire from the CNR. He said he would meet me in Windsor and we could drive back together. My new friend, Joe, said if I was going that far I should continue on to New York and he would try to meet me there.

It was January and I still had my hockey players but Dorothy, once again, said she would take care of things. Soon I was on my way, stopping in New Westminster to stay with my sister and her husband for a few days. Betty's husband, Gordon, was a great guy. He arranged for a hotel in New York. "While you're in New York," he cautioned me, "Don't look up or act like a tourist."

Gordon took me to the airport and put a bunch of

quarters in my hand, saying "These are for the doorman and taxi drivers." One of my hockey players gave me his aunt's phone number, telling me to be sure to call her.

I was on my way to New York! My first time in that wonderful city! Several hours later I looked down to see the Hudson River below. I couldn't believe what I saw below-it was a huge cemetery. I learned later that Woodlawn Cemetery in Van Cortland Park is 300 acres in which 300,000 people are buried.

It was a crisp, cold winter day when I arrived. The trees were bare and I must admit I felt just a little nervous, a small town girl alone in this big city.

A message was waiting for me when I arrived at my hotel to say that my friend, Joe, would not be in New York for two days. I wasn't going to waste one minute of my time in New York, so I took a cab to the United Nations, remembering to tip the driver with some of Gordon's quarters. I tried hard not to look up or act like a tourist but, I must admit, I did my share of staring up at the skyscrapers around me and the crowds of people on the sidewalks. At the U.N. I met another lady on her own. She was from Boston and we soon discovered she wasn't staying too far from my hotel. We decided to have dinner together. I've always found that you don't have to be lonely, on your own and I've met some really interesting people in my travels. Sometimes, just to share what would ordinarily be a lonely meal, is enough.

Then Joe came and he did spoil me. He showed me New York at night, taking me to the famous Stork Club, where he knew the owner, and the Twenty-one. Joe was very generous and I could see he was having fun showing New York to me. We drank champagne and ate caviar. We saw the famous Rockettes and all the latest shows as well. I could hardly believe that I was in New York and there, on the stage, was Mary Martin in South Pacific! I sensed that Joe was not the marrying kind and that suited me just fine. We never talked seriously about our lives and he never told me much about himself, but I sensed that there was some sadness in his life that he was just glad to forget for awhile. Over the years, running the Mayfair, I saw quite a few guys like Joe. That was when I learned that however tough you think your life is, there are always plenty of people who are worse off.

At the end of my time in New York, Joe said, "Why don't you drive to Florida instead of going back across Canada?" He thought it would make more sense to head south and drive across the southern states to California and then back up the coast to home. Of course, that route could mean a stop in Medford to see him. It was tempting. It was still cold in Kamloops, so I decided to follow his advice. I'll always be grateful to Joe. Because of his suggestion, my life was about to change forever.

Uncle Ben was waiting for me in Windsor, with our golf clubs when I arrived there. He, of course, had travelled across the country by train on his lifetime pass. I was about to pick up my first car.

We drove the new car heading south through the border and into Detroit, on our way to Florida and sunshine. We were through the city and into the suburbs when it started to get dark. I had been so eager to get behind the wheel and start living my new life we hadn't even checked where the lights were in the car when we picked it up at the factory. As darkness fell, we pulled off the road and into a driveway to try to find the headlight switch. Suddenly there were lights everywhere and the deafening sound of what seemed like a hundred barking dogs; unfriendly lights and unfriendly dogs; dogs nothing like my little Fritzi. Dogs trained to bring intruders to the ground. A gentleman came down to the car and greeted us cautiously. He listened while we told him our improbable story, that we had driven our brand new car away from the factory without evening knowing how to turn on the headlights. It turned out that he was an executive of General Motors. When he saw we were driving one of his cars he invited us in, found us a place to stay for the night and gave us a tour of our new car. Once he made sure we knew how to operate the car's many accessories, he told us the best route to take to Florida. The next morning Ben and I were on our way south exploring new territory. We were in no hurry, Ben celebrating his hard won freedom from work and I, celebrating my freedom from Jack and my newly discovered faith in myself. The motel was in good hands. We were on a holiday. It seems we took quite awhile to get to Florida.

Our joy ride came to a gentle stop in Hollywood

Beach. It was George Washington's birthday. That we weren't the only tourists in town is an understatement. When we finally found a place to stay, although there were no bedbugs, it was not up to my standards and neither was it on the beach. The woman owner of the place where we had wanted to stay took our names, and said, "Come back tomorrow and I'll have a suite for you." When we checked in the next day I told her I was in the same business in a small way, so she gave us a good rate and showed me around the place. I found that when I introduced myself as a fellow motel operator, other owners were eager to show me around their places and often gave me a preferred rate.

At that moment, I noticed a tall, good-looking man standing in the office. He stepped aside, while I registered Ben and myself. When I went back to our unit, the door was locked and I hollered, "Uncle Ben where are you?" Who should step out of the next unit but the handsome man I had seen in the office. I fell in love with him right at that moment.

He said with a smile, "He's in here with me. Come on in". He and Ben were having a drink but he didn't offer me one. He introduced himself as Ted. Later he told me his name was Wilfred Steadman Thompson. "Ted" seemed nicer, certainly less formal. Uncle Ben said, "Would you like a drink Margaret?" "Sherry?" Ted asked.

Later he told me he had been accused of teaching

one woman to drink and he wasn't going to be accused again. The woman was his wife and she became an alcoholic.

Ted asked us to join him for dinner and later we played Jai Alai. "Will I see you tomorrow?" he asked as we said goodnight. We agreed to meet for a day at the beach.

I've always loved to swim. The water was warm and just pleasantly salty, as Ted and I swam out side by side through the waves. I could see that he was a strong swimmer and I couldn't help noticing his tanned, athletic legs and broad shoulders.

Suddenly my arm was on fire. First my arm and then my back. I started screaming the pain was so excruciating. We were right in the middle of several bright blue jellyfish—a school of dangerous Portuguese Man of War. They were stinging us both but Ted, luckily, managed to escape with just a few stings. I was covered with them. I swam for shore frantically. Ted swam beside me and when the water was shallow enough for us to stand, he scooped me up and carried me out. He could see by now that I had red welts on my arms, my face and even up my nose.

"I must get you to the hospital," he said. Leaving Uncle Ben on the beach, he carried me back to the motel where the motel owner wrapped me in fresh white towels and called a doctor for us.

Many years after my darling Ted died, I found the travel diary he kept during those wonderful weeks after we first met. I found it in a drawer with his fez and some other Masonic belongings. It brought back so many memories. It was if he was standing beside me again. Perhaps he was.

He decided to leave his car in storage at Hollywood Beach and come along with us across the country on our way home to Kamloops. I'm going to let him tell the next part of the story.

"Checked in at Meridian Motel. Noon – noticed attractive girl in office – over heard she was from B.C. – so while unpacking my luggage as was the fellow next door – noted the car from B.C. ________ I invite him in for a long cool drink after our long and tiring labour in the hot sun. Of course he was kind enough to introduce me to his daughter – later we went for a swim and sun on the beach. I found out that Margaret is single – likes to play golf – so we all dine at Sherry's and then to Jai Ali which we all enjoyed. Though no money was made, friends were made.

Thursday

Swim and sun in a.m. -very warm and nice – 100 yards from beach. Dropped in on old friends and then went to Old Scandia for a smorgasbord style dinner in quaint old country surroundings. Sun and beach in a.m. Golf with Margaret in p.m. She plays a very good game and knows all the rules. Went for swim on our return about 3:30 p.m. The swimming was fine but about 100 yards out we ran into a school of

Portuguese Man of War – a jelly fish thing with long 15 or 20 foot tentacles – fine thread like strands with small blue beads – and each bead a string. Margaret screamed. I swam toward her and as I threw or splashed two away she cried "It's like fire". I felt a few stings. We swam ashore. Her arms were crisscrossed with stings.

We went to the office of a nearby motel. The people there suggested ammonia to neutralize the acid but it did not have much effect. Her back seemed paralyzed so she went to a doctor who agreed it was very bad but did not seem to know what to do about it. He painted it with metaphen and bandaged it and also gave her some kind of a hypo. No results – not even sedative. Later I went back to ask him for something to deaden the pain for her.

Margaret stayed in bed and rested for three days. The burning sensation was still very severe. The stings looked like whiplashes. I had about one foot of stings while she must have had 20 feet, and all fire I'll vouch.

We had planned to go night clubbing – no Miami moon for us tonight but she thought my bedside manner very consoling. Much nicer than the doctor. I surprised her with a great big ice cream sundae, topped with a big red cherry. The way to a woman's heart......

Saturday

Drove to Fort Lauderdale to call on friends. Dinner at Bahai Mar Yacht Club, spent evening with Margaret. The welts are still fire red.

Sunday

Just swimming in the pool no beach. Miami papers printed

warnings of numerous "Man of War" on beaches – about one inch on inside page. Sort of nurse maid. Sunday beach traffic is too heavy to drive in so it is best to stay near the pool. Sunday dinner at Gallagher.

Monday

Margaret feels better but could not sleep. We went to Hileah Raceway. Wanted to go in the new club house but a coat is required. So after some talk rented one from an attendant who happened to have some coats hidden in the bushes. Later when we wanted to lunch the coat would not fit me and I could not just carry it on my arm as I had done to get past the gate so were refused admission. Went to "Jamaica Inn" for dinner in Key Biscayne – a very lovely place with a large glass enclosed tropical garden with all kinds of flowers and plants. Orchids, breadfruit trees, bananas, palms, etc. Very lush and tropical. Food good and reasonable. Later, moon light and Margaret! We went dancing after taking Uncle Ben home. She can dance!

Tuesday

Swim in pool and sun. Drive to Parrot Jungle. Beautiful landscaped garden and pool with fountain. Walk through arbor with birds from all over the world. The attendant puts on an interesting show with parrots who will do his bidding. About 200 flamingos, striding and running about. I am invited to New Orleans with Margaret and Ben Miller – in their car and fly back here.

Wednesday

Of course I accepted. We stopped at Tampa "Bamboo Inn". Drove out Tamiami Trail, then on to Everglade country

– many herons and cranes etc. all along. Drove up west coast to Tampa in a hurricane. Rain and wind. The papers said winds up to 75 mph. Rain and blowing so hard we had to stop car at times. Good it was a new Cadillac and did not leak.

Thursday

Drove on to Panama City, "the world's finest beach". The beach is fine with white sand. This is their off season-too cold here in winter but inland people come during the summer months. Dined in a nice place and had it all to ourselves. I put a nickel in the Juke Box so we could have a dance. Her arm is better but still aches and didn't stop her from dancing with me. She can dance!

Friday

Drove to Pass Christian, 60 miles from New Orleans. Made arrangements at motel, then drove into city. We feared we could not get motel without reservations – they must have over-advertised for we stopped and found vacancies at several. So made arrangements to move into the city next day. Margaret told the clerk we would stay 4 or 5 days if he could get us tickets to a New Orleans Ball – dined and drove around the city – Got a city map etc. then back to Pass Christian.

Saturday

Desk clerk got us tickets for "Debutantes' Ball" sponsored by the Shriners – formal dress so I rented a tuxedo and was fortunate enough to find black shoes, size 13 – Margaret had a black dress with white Belgian lace. Tickets were admission only, so we were there early - were in balcony. Evening clothes made no difference. Everyone running and fighting for a seat – women wanting to hold a whole row – and angry if you came near them. We finally got seated and I went down to the main floor and talked with a couple of Shriners in their oriental costumes and was given seats on the main floor next to the queen's box among the elite of New Orleans. The Shriners enacted a pageant with water scenes of various fish. Costumes very colourful and elaborate. The princess and her several attendants – (all debutantes) were beautifully gowned. Last year's belles were present. After the pageantry is over the actors are permitted to "call" for previously arranged partners to dance. These are the only people allowed to dance so to be on someone's "call" list is an honor. Later dancing is permitted.

Wednesday, March 17

St. Patrick's Day A fine evening: Margaret and I went to the "Chef's Inn". They had Irish party favours and a sing-along of all the good old Irish ballads. The food was excellent, and after dinner Margaret and I danced.

Friday, March 19

I'm getting pressed for time – this vacation must end sometime.

Sunday, 21st

Margaret and Ben left for San Francisco this morning, so my pleasant journey across the country ends. I have enjoyed the company of these people very much. Tonight my plane leaves for Miami.

As we drove across the continent that spring Ted gradually told me about himself. He lived in Presque Isle, Maine with his mother. Well educated, he was a pharmacist who owned his own business. His father, also a pharmacist, was no longer alive. His wife was an alcoholic and, after many sad long years of trying unsuccessfully to help her, they divorced. He had been on his own for five years. His two youngest daughters were married with children of their own and he was returning to Maine for the wedding of his eldest daughter. When I first met him, I noticed he was wearing a Shriner's ring. I remember thinking to myself, "If he's a Shriner, he can't be all bad." My old friend, Earl was a Shriner, too, and I knew the Shriners worked hard for good causes—in particular, setting up hospitals and treatment for children.

What an understatement that was. After spending those wonderful weeks with him, I couldn't think of anything bad about him. As far as I was concerned he was the best. We had so much in common. We were both curious and loved to travel. We loved dancing and good food. Just being together was so comfortable.

Ted and I went out for dinner on our last night together. Before we left, Uncle Ben asked Ted, "Isn't this the last supper?"

Ted replied, "No. I will be coming out to Kamloops to see how the fishing is."

"Au revoir, then," Uncle Ben said, shaking hands with Ted, leaving us to have dinner alone together and to say our goodbyes.

"Margaret," Ted said taking my hand, "Let's have one last swim."

We were staying in a beautiful ocean front motel Each unit had it's own deck almost right at the water's edge. The surf was gentle that evening, the stars bright above us. We were both quiet, knowing our make-believe affair was at an end. Some real decisions were ahead of us.

"Too bad Ted lives so far away," Uncle Ben remarked one day to me. I knew that the miles separating us were not the only obstacle to our relationship. I had the motel and several employees to concern me. Ted had his family and business back in Maine.

I knew I loved Ted but I was afraid. Afraid of making another mistake like my marriage to Jack. And yet, I knew now that Ted was nothing like Jack. He was kind, patient, fun, and easy to be with.

I'd known other men since Jack. I had never even been tempted to get serious with any of them. Not even Joe. I had been so badly scarred by my years with Jack. I was determined never to be dependent on any man again.

We swam out lazily, easily over the surf and lay on our backs looking at the stars. The water was warm. I felt so easy and relaxed as we swam in again. I know that both of us were remembering that first day on the beach back in Florida when Ted carried me out of the water.

We sat side by side, watching the moon rise over the Pacific.

"Margaret," Ted said softly.

Suddenly I was in his arms and he was kissing me, gently at first but then urgently. I could taste the salt on his lips as he carried me into his room. I forgot all my worries in my desire for him. Nothing else mattered. We were together and one.

As Uncle Ben and I headed north up Highway 1, I couldn't get over the size of California. It seemed as if we had been driving for ever. I was on cloud nine because I knew that Ted and I would soon be together again. I had given him my sister's address in New Westminister and, because I was sure he would write to me there, Uncle Ben and I didn't waste too much time getting home. If Ted's letter was waiting for me at Betty's, I would know that the past few weeks and especially that last night hadn't been a dream.

We only made a few stops on the way up the coast on Highway One, the only road north before the construction of the I5. Stopping only to see the Hearst Castle, and staying just long enough on the Monterey Peninsula to know I had to return someday, we travelled up Oregon's rugged coast and inland up the Columbia River. All my thoughts, I must admit, centred on Ted. We had only been separated a few short days but how I missed him! I couldn't believe my desire for him. It was as if all my senses had been awakened on that last night in California. I had never felt like this before. I kept thinking about Ted's blue eyes and dark hair. Was he really over six feet tall? I felt so wonderful in his arms, especially on the dance floor. Could I remember his voice? Would he call me at Betty's? On and on.

Uncle Ben could see I was preoccupied and eager to get home.

"You've found the right one, now, Margaret," was all he needed to say.

When we arrived at my sister's, sure enough a couple of letters were waiting for me. It was now the end of March and spring comes early in the west, so we headed back to Kamloops to be ready for the opening of the tourist season. Of course I told Betty about Ted. I remember she said to me, thoughtfully, "But, Margaret, you're in love with a man who lives at least 3,000 miles away! Neither of you will want to give up your business." I knew that she thought I was once again being a dreamer, not practical, ruled by my heart. That kind of thinking led to all my troubles with Jack. My first marriage was a disaster. Was I about to do something impetuous again?

Ted was coming in May. Until I heard the news I was on cloud nine. Ben and I hadn't been home a week, when I received a phone call asking if I'd heard the news about the plane crash. Gordon, my wonderful brother-in-law, was dead. Two planes collided in mid air over

Moosejaw, crashing to the ground, narrowly missing a school and killing everyone onboard. No one seemed to know how it happened. It was April 8th, 1954, a beautiful spring day.

I was on the next plane out of Kamloops back to New Westminster to be with my sister. I couldn't help but think of the last time I saw Gordon, remembering his advice, "Don't look up and don't look like a tourist!" as I flew off to New York.

Betty was numb with grief. Gordon was dead and she was alone with their two children, Carol who was 13 and Keath who was 7. I suppose for their sakes she managed to pull herself together. She was a brick and she did have a funny bone. She said through her tears "I guess now I can get rid of the stinky cheese." Gordon's love of Limburger was a joke between us all. The hardest time was waiting for the authorities to send Gordon's body back. The horror was complete when the sealed coffin arrived in New Westminster. Black letters on the top said, "Head". So many people attended Gordon's funeral and somehow we got through it.

We had to go on. When I went back to Kamloops after the funeral, I hated to leave Betty. We spent many long hours talking about what she would do with Gordon gone but she had good friends, and two children to look after. We had both faced up to challenges before and both of us found inner strengths to sustain us. Even so, I don't know how she got through the days.

Ted arrived at the end of May. Just before he left Boston he stopped at a jeweller's and bought me a gold charm bracelet with a lobster on it. It was the first of many charms he gave me over the years, each one marking a special event or a special place in our lives together. By the time he returned to Maine at the end of June he asked me to come to Maine in the fall and meet his family.

Once again, I'll let him tell the story of his trip to Kamloops.

May 25, 1954

After seven weeks home am off to Vancouver. Always wanted to see the Northeast. It may be delayed wanderlust or "cherchez la femme". In Boston, I went for a long walk to Tremont Street where I bought a charm for Margaret's bracelet- a lobster with moveable claws. Quiet atmosphere, sedate and regal – you are treated like a gentleman. "Shall I charge it?"

Plane to Montreal at 5 p.m. Interesting, flat country with many lakes, after crossing the White Mountains. Customs at Montreal, then plane at 8 p.m., all night to Vancouver.

Thursday, May 27

Arrived at 6 a.m. Went downtown for lunch and shopping, but stores all closed on Wednesday, so caught the next plane out of Vancouver to Kamloops and arrived at 3 p.m. to an awaiting Margaret and Ben Miller with a smile like a new moon.

"God," I said. "Am I glad to see you! I told you in California that it would not be the last supper and now I'm here!"

Margaret has a nice motel (motor courts in Canada) 12 units and fixed up excellent, some have light housekeeping.

Kamloops is in the Thompson River Valley. 1200 feet and very dry, dusty, warm, even sagebrush. It is several mountain ranges from the coast which stop the rain. Apples, peaches, pears, hops are grown here at the rail junction of both the Canadian Pacific and the Canadian National railways. The population is about 12,000 people and it is a nice small town (4 drugstores).

The Shrine Temple of Vancouver had a parade and ceremonial and ball in the ice arena. Nearly 1,000 there- all the best of Kamloops and Margaret made a lovely impression on her friends as well as myself. Met several small nobles and had steaks with them.

Saturday night we went to Margaret's camp at Paul Lake- 15 miles from Kamloops. Lovely setting for her nice camp.

Ben is a finishing carpenter. Back Sunday night. Margaret caught three trout, Ted, 0. I rowed the boat. First met Tom O'Brien and Bill Smtih of Vancouver (Shriners). More later.

Stayed till Wednesday in Kamloops. Drove around a bit, met several friends of Margaret's. Drove up to Shuswap Lake and Salmon Arm. Lovely lodge. We ate dinner, also ate at Echo Lodge, Paul Lake- established for many years and good fishing.

Left for Rotary International Convention at Seattle, June 6th. Drove down Fraser River Canyon. Very scenic drive following the river, sometimes at river's edge, at other times a thousand feet above, among mountains four or five thousand feet. Stayed two days at Harrison Hot Springs, "The Spa of Canada", a year round hotel with hot sulfur waters. We swam in the pool which warns you that after 15 minutes may be very tiring. Good food and dancing in the "Copper Room" – large fireplace and finishings all of polished copper.

Rained all the way down, lunched at Boston Bar (the name intrigued me). Gold years ago, now good fishing for steelhead. Met friend of Margaret's who gathers and polishes agates and sells semi-precious stones – agates, jade, etc. which she finds in this section. Drove through Chilliwack Valley, cherry center of the world. Festival, later to Vancouver. A real fine, clean city. Nice hotels and stores. I stayed on the way up at Hotel Vancouver, Like the Chateau Frontenac in Quebec.

Met and stayed with Margaret's sister, Betty, who recently lost her husband in a plane crash. She has a lovely home and a boy and girl, and is very talented in art. Nice painting and ceramic work. Danced and danced at the Hotel Vancouver with Betty and Muriel and Lawrence Swanson. Then drove miles Sunday to Seattle.

Sunday, June 6th

Reservations at new Washington Hotel for Rotary convention. Registered at convention and spent sometime in "The Hall of Friendship", a meeting place for Rotarians – writing desks and easy chairs. Margaret met and was impressed by a Sikh from Pakistan with his turban and jeweled, gold brocade jacket and turned up shoes. That evening, we attended the Seattle Symphonic Orchestra program in the civic auditorium and we were ushered to seats next to the Sikh, so I nobly suggested that Margaret sit next to him and converse with him to find out what princes, etc., do in Pakistan. After some small attempt to talk during which time he was very uneasy and fidgety in his seat, he left although the program was not half over. When he had gone,

I asked why and she replied "He stinks!" However the concert was very nice and had several choral groups who were very good.

We attended the first meeting of Rotary International. All meetings were interesting with good speakers. Choral groups spiced it up. Rotarians went all out to entertain. Outdoor salmon bake, boat rides. We were invited to Dr. Richard Fuller's home. He is very wealthy. He gave the city of Seattle its art museum. About thirty of us – a wonderful dinner, served to perfection.

Tuesday

Dining out at nice places, finding a dance or two. Driving around lovely homes on the shore of Lake Washington. Meeting and getting acquainted with many Rotarians.

Friday, June 11th

The Pacific Northwest Shrine Association moved into town. With all their color and garbs, three mounted horse patrols. They had three burrows in the Hotel Olympic and were angry that they could not ride them up and down the elevators. The parade was excellent and the ceremonial in the auditorium was put on and carried out as well as any stage production.

Saturday, June 12th

Drove to Mount Rainier Saturday. At the 5,500 level. There were twenty feet of snow against the lodge. The road has just been opened. Saturday night and the town full of Shriners. Drums and noise and the streets and in the hotel corridors. Dined and danced, and to bed early.

Sunday, June 13th

7 a.m. Up early to catch ferry boat to Victoria, through

the Strait of Juan de Fuca. Impressive approach to the city, right up in front of Empress Hotel, all covered in ivy, beautiful landscaping about grounds with Victoria spelled out in flowers. Really quaint English city, and they want to keep it that way. Many shops with china, linens, woolens. Tea is served at 4 p.m. in the lobby of the Empress. Run by the C.P.R. Stopped with friends of Margaret's for tea.

Drove around coastal roads with many lovely homes with lovely flowers. Mostly retired people from all over Canada.

Then Monday, a drive to Campbell River Fishing Lodge (Painter's Lodge). Saw deer and partridge with six young ones, and was arrested for speeding (70 mph) at Ladysmith. Appeared before magistrate with court opened by Canadian Mountie for "Her Majesty the Queen". Very formal and English.

Tuesday, June 14

Stayed at Painter's Lodge last night and were fishing Monday for 20 or 30lb. Pacific salmon. "Springs" were supposed to be here, but evidently not too many, because one 17-pounder was the only one caught. July and August are the best months, and reservations booked far in advance. Fish up to 70 lbs. are caught. But none were around when we were. Caught several ling cod. Lovely lodge and nice people. Would like to return. Fish in the a.m., then to Vancouver, stayed in motel, contacted T.D. O'Brien and played golf at the exclusive Capilano. Beautiful club house and grounds surrounded by lovely homes in British properties financed by Guinness money. Lots at $400 and up and homes landscaped beautifully. Anything can be grown in Vancouver. Rock gardens are wonderful.

Spent a nice evening with the O'Briens and Smiths (met in Kamloops), in their lovely home - $7,500?

Called on friends in Vancouver. Drove about city, some shopping. Visited with Betty Hutton and on our way to Penticton, through Alison Pass saw snow back among the trees at this late date.

June 17th

Golf at Penticton in the Okanagan Valley, famous for its apples and peaches. Then across Okanagan Lake to Kelowna- a quiet English town. We saw bowling on the green and then to Kamloops, arriving Saturday night to be welcomed by Ben Miller.

Sunday

Drove 40 miles to Douglas Lake Cattle Company ranch, largest except for King Ranch in Texas. To Salmon Lake. Shelters, tents and cabins – you do your own cooking etc. Fishing for 2-3 lb. trout. The Kamloops trout very bright and silvery, not as dark as ours. Here you can catch all you wish. You are allowed 24 per day or 48 in all, and you can catch that many if you wish. They fight well and taste great.

Drove back Monday and started preparations for the trip back to Presque Isle.

Left Kamloops Tuesday, 3 p.m. and Vancouver at 8 p.m. Lovely sunset and could still see pink clouds of the sunset. Just an ordinary flight to Saskatoon, Winnipeg, Toronto and New York. Then North East Airlines to Presque Isle at midnight.

In the past three months I have been in Maine, Florida, California, Washington and British Columbia.

That summer was the busiest one yet. People from the States had discovered Kamloops and the interior of B.C., but we still had many folks from Victoria and the

Vancouver area. It is much sunnier in the interior and people liked to escape the rainfall on the coast by coming up to see us. The Mayfair Auto Court was full most of the time. One thing I learned, being in the motor hotel business, is you must always have a smile on your face no matter how tired you are. Try to be helpful, know your area, and be ready to answer questions. In my case, that meant being knowledgeable about fishing conditions. Knowing how to catch the best fish always served me well. I did enjoy meeting new people every day, driving my dream car and spending as much time as I could on the golf course. Ted was never far from my thoughts. I was going to have to make some serious decisions before long, but right now, I just wanted to think about how much I loved being with him and how much I was missing him.

Chapter 5

My New Family

In the fall, as I made plans to go to Maine, to see Ted and meet his daughters and his mother, a letter arrived from Ted with a cheque for my plane fare. Of course, I didn't need the money and I couldn't accept it. If I went back there, it would be on my own money. Ted understood I needed to meet his family on my own terms. I wanted to be independent. I wondered, though, if he really understood me? What would it be like to be Ted's wife? Could I give up my hard-earned freedom to do with my life as I pleased?

I decided to leave my worries in Kamloops. The travel bug had bitten me and I loved to fly. I was off to Maine! Ted's eldest daughter, Eileen, met me at the airport. I liked her right away. Ted was at a meeting so Eileen and I had lunch together and a chance to get to know each other. She said she was so happy that Ted had found me. She told me about the years Ted tried to cope with her mother's alcoholism. She said he was always finding bottles of liquor hidden around the house which was such a mess. It must have been very difficult to share this with me. Later, when we met Ted at the hotel, it made things much easier that Eileen and I had spent some time together.

The next day we drove north to Maine just as the leaves were beginning to show their beautiful fall colours. Before going on to Presque Isle, we stopped at Rockport, Maine where Ted attended a pharmacists' convention. It was my first taste of what life would be like if Ted and I decided to marry. We played golf and went dancing. Ted asked me to bring the dress I wore to the ball in New Orleans, a beautiful strapless dress of white Belgian lace and black tulle. Ted whispered "You're a knockout!" as he proudly introduced me to several of his associates. Everyone was friendly, disproving what I had heard about New Englanders—that they viewed newcomers with suspicion, especially if you hadn't been there since the Mayflower landed. I knew Ted's friends and associates were happy to see that Ted was enjoying life again.

After the convention we drove north to Presque Isle. The closer we got to Ted's place, the more anxious I became. In fact, I was scared stiff. What would Ted's mother think of me? How much had he told her? I knew their family tree had roots far back in the history of Maine, and also, that everyone in the family was well educated. I had never even finished high school, and although father's family had once been well to do, Betty and I, at one point, literally hadn't a dime between us. I remember Ted pulled the car over, took my hand and said, "Relax, they'll love you as much as I do! And as for the family pedigree, forget it. You are the exotic flower here in Maine—a westerner from cattle country and a spunky girl with her own business. As for the education, just tell them you graduated from Whidapitlock U.

They'll never know the difference. You're the best example of a self-educated person I've ever met. OK, now?" I nodded and we pulled back onto the highway.

Ted was right. His mother was a darling. I loved her on sight. She lived in a wonderful old heritage house, over 150 years old. She welcomed me warmly and soon let me know that she approved of our plans. Her husband had died several years ago, some time before Ted came back to live with her. She told me she didn't mind a bit that Ted would be leaving. "It's about time he had some happiness," she told me.

Ted's mother had more than her share of sadness, also. Ted's youngest brother was killed while playing with dynamite caps. She and her husband were on holiday at the time. She arrived home moments before the boy died.

Ted took time off to take me around Aroostook County. As Pharmacy Commissioner for the state, he had to visit all the drug stores in Maine. It is full of lovely lakes and, at that time of the year, their still waters reflected all the glory of every sunny autumn day. I was learning all about Maine, with Ted, my knowledgeable guide. He was eager to show me his country just as I had enjoyed introducing him to B.C. Lumber, seed potatoes and tourism were then the sources of most of Maine's economy. With all of its many bays, coves and inlets, it has one of the longest and most beautiful coastlines in the country. My thoughts went back the trip up the west coast Uncle Ben and I drove just a few months before. I remember being eager to get back to Betty's place so see if there was a letter from Ted. Now here I was sitting beside him in the car, discovering things about him that made me love him more and more.

One day we flew into a beautiful lake resort and stayed in one of just two secluded lodges. A guide came every morning to light the fire in our cottage. It was idyllic, having an early morning coffee in front of a cosy log fire. We soon decided that after we were married, no matter where we were or how busy, we would always begin each day together like this.

One day, while having a meal at the main lodge, Ted Williams came in. I had no idea who he was. Hockey, not baseball, was my only spectator sport back in Kamloops. Ted loved to fish so we had quite a chat. I told him about Kamloops trout and said he must come and try the fishing in B.C.

The days seemed to be flying past. I knew I had to get back to Kamloops and the auto court. I knew Dorothy and Janet were doing a good job of running the business while I was away, but there are some things a small business owner just can't leave to others.

Before we left, standing in front of a glowing fire in his mother's beautiful living room, Ted again asked me to marry him. Of course, I said yes, knowing that there were some major hurdles to jump before we could be together. The first was to divorce Jack. We were legally separated but neither of us had bothered to take the separation to its logical conclusion. Ted's mother, who was delighted that we were going to marry, said "You had better get down to Reno and get that divorce."

Back in B.C., I stopped to see how Betty was doing. I was uneasy about a man she was seeing. I couldn't put my finger on it, but there was something about him I just didn't feel comfortable with. I didn't say anything to Betty but kept my thoughts to myself. In Kamloops, I praised Janet and Dorothy for taking care of things so well while I was away. I knew that without them, I could never have spent so much time travelling that year. I think working at the motel kept Dorothy from thinking too much about Les.

It was strange but a couple from Reno had left their luggage at the court and when they returned the next day, I told them I was planning to go to Reno to obtain my divorce. They were also motel owners. Meeting them was heaven-sent. They said they would give me a good rate at their place. They met me at the airport when I flew down and drove me to their place, the Casa Laguna Motel. It worked out well for them, too. When they wanted to go out, I took care of the office for them.

It's hard for people today to understand how difficult it was to get a divorce in Canada back in the 1950's. In those days, without proof of adultery—your partner's, you were out of luck. It was a long and costly process, which included both hiring a lawyer and also a private detective who specialized in catching people in the act of adultery. Of course, many of these incidents were staged, and were both embarrassing and demoralizing, but necessary if you wanted out of a bad relationship. Nobody spoke of wife abuse back then, either. So, even if someone had caught Jack in one of his rages, it would not have helped in a divorce suit. It was years before divorce was made easier and women were granted legal protection from abuse.

On the other hand, it was easy to get a divorce in Reno. All you needed was money. Many Canadians flew down to Nevada, where you had to stay six weeks, return home and fly back for two or three weeks. The cost was $1,000, $500 the first visit and another $500 the second. Then you received divorce papers that were valid only in the States. If you remarried and returned to live in Canada, you could be charged with bigamy.

Six weeks was a long time to be alone in a strange town. Reno was a little place with one long Main Street on the Truckee River, high up in the Sierra Nevada mountains. The Casa Laguna was right on the river.

I made friends with another girl staying there who was also waiting for a divorce from an abusive husband. She had children and told me that, because of them, she had tried to put up with her husband. Finally, she couldn't stand it any more and left him. We spent a lot of time together. Both our units had kitchens so we took turns cooking. We also met a fellow who took us out together for meals and to the movies. We found out that he never did take a woman out on her own—safety in numbers, I guess! He also taught us how to play poker.

Ted phoned every day and he, also, taught me the finer points of poker playing over the phone. Hearing his voice reassured me about the decision I had taken to leave my business, friends and family to marry him. I lived for his letters. Every day someone would walk up to the highway, collect the mail and bring it down to our motel. Ted wrote every day.

We made a few trips out of town, visiting places like Carson City and the Bucket of Blood Saloon, and somehow the days passed. At Christmas I went back to Kamloops, stopping at Betty's on the way to reassure myself that she was all right. A quick return to Reno to pick up my divorce papers and I was on a plane for Seattle, where Betty, Carol and Uncle Ben met me at the airport.

Chapter 6

A New Life With Ted

When Ted arrived in Seattle, I was never so glad to see anyone. We were married in church the next day. I wore a blue silk dress with a mink stole and carried two white orchids. It was a lovely, simple ceremony. I looked at Ted, handsome in a grey suit. It was a dream come true. There was more to come.

Our wedding, Margaret and Ted.

We flew to Hawaii for our honeymoon. At first it was not idyllic. We stayed at the Biltmore, then under construction. Jackhammers instead of soft Hawaiian music filled the air on our first morning. We decided to move. In 1955 there were not many large hotels in Hawaii so we stayed at Neamola, a small place owned by an old sea captain. While we were there Edgar Kaiser offered the old man a million dollars for it. Kaiser later turned it into the Hawaiian Village. It had lovely little cottages in a lush tropical garden. Each cottage had its own electric plate so we had that wonderful Kona coffee every morning before walking up past Fort De Roosey to the Halekalani (House Without a Key) hotel for our favourite breakfast of fresh pineapple and the most delicious pancakes I had ever tasted. They also served a wonderful fresh coconut cream pie. During the day we went sightseeing, spent time at the beach or in our pool. Every night we danced by torchlight.

We took a four-island tour. We had a car with a driver on each island and even had a guide with a ukulele. The tour guide picked hibiscus flowers for me, saying to Ted, "Now you must kiss your bride! That is the custom here in the islands."

Both Ted and I just naturally liked people. Both his work in the pharmacy business and mine in the auto court helped us quickly establish a rapport with new acquaintances. Often, as happened in Hawaii, those acquaintances became friends. One day we met a young

Our honeymoon in Hawaii.

woman, who was head of the WACs, stationed in Honolulu. Her parents were visiting her and she was driving them around the island, showing them the sights. Because she was on duty much of the time, she asked us if we would be tour guides for her mother and father. She would be delighted to lend us her car with its official seal, enabling us to enter the military bases and even to go down into a submarine. I didn't like it down there one bit and couldn't help but admire those seamen who serve in those undersea vessels for months at a time. Years later, I met a submarine commander of twenty-five years. He taught me how to walk, head up straight ahead.

When it was time to board the Luraline to sail back to the mainland, many of our new friends gathered on the dock, each with a lei to put around our necks as they said goodbye. "Throw them in the water as you sail for home," they said, smiling. "If they drift towards the shore, you'll surely return to Hawaii." It must be true, because I have been back many times to the islands and I always love it.

The Royal Hawaiian Band played as we sailed away to San Francisco. Ted had reserved an entire suite aboard, a living room, bedroom and bathroom.

Instead of flying back to Maine, when we arrived in San Francisco, we flew up to Vancouver to see Betty's new cottage at Belcarra Park. Art George took us in his water taxi across the inlet, from North Vancouver to Belcarra. The trip seemed to take for ever and I began to worry because this was, after all his business and he was waiting to take us back. "Don't worry," Betty told me. "He won't mind waiting. He likes me." She was right about that. Sure enough, Betty and Art were married in November.

Finally, for Ted and me, the honeymoon was over and we were on our way back to Maine where the real world awaited us. At first, we stayed with his mother. Of course, Ted was busy with his work and, I must admit, I found it hard to adjust. No longer an independent business woman, I was now known only as Ted's wife. I missed the Mayfair and my life in Kamloops. And as much as I loved Ted's mother, I longed for a home of my own but we would have to do a lot of looking before we found the right house.

Ted was very understanding. How different from Jack! He suggested a trip to the Gaspé through small, quaint French Canadian villages dominated by tall white church spires. We stopped to watch the craftsmen carve exquisite wooden figures and bought some as souvenirs of our trip. We stayed in Quebec City, where the beautiful Chateau Frontenac looks down over the old town and out over the majestic St. Lawrence River. We

Fishing on the Gaspé.

visited St. Anne de Beaupré and saw the rows and rows of crutches lining the walls of the shrine there. Crutches of believers who had not been able to walk, and, after praying to the saint, walked away leaving their crutches behind forever.

Our last stop was Montreal, also an old city but with the modern, sophisticated feel of a busy, European metropolis. The French Canadians had such 'joie de vivre'! One day we went shopping at Ogilvie's, a department store owned at that time by an old established Scots family. The store opening was announced by a bagpiper, piping down though the store's many departments.

We were still very much in love, but, looking into the future, we had a lot to do.

When we returned, there was the matter of my green card. Although I was now married to an American, I needed a green card to stay in the country. To get a green card, I had to apply from outside the U.S., so back I went to Vancouver, to fill in more papers, produce a birth certificate, be fingerprinted and wait for permission to join Ted, once again. There was still more waiting, this time for the green card to arrive in the mail. It never did come. Finally I left without it.

It was during this process that I realized there was confusion about my birth date. My birth certificate said November second. Father always told me I was born on

November fourth. I'm sure the fact that my mother was gravely ill at the time accounts for his confusion.

I sold my treasured blue Cadillac to my new brother-in-law, Art George. Ted had arranged for me to pick up a new one in Detroit, where he would be waiting when I left the West Coast. We both hoped this was the last time we would be apart.

As I handed the car keys to Art, I remembered Uncle Ben teaching me how to drive in Kamloops. He drove a Roadmaster Buick, given to him by Imperial Oil. They sent him down to Peru to oversee the change over of railway engines down there from coal to oil, and gave him the Buick as a thank you when he returned. Funny how things do come around. My father lost his fortune when the gas lamps on city streets in England became electric.

Uncle Ben's Roadmaster Buick.

Jack refused to let me practice on his truck but, by then, I would have been too nervous to learn anything from him anyway. Road rage supposedly is a sign of our hectic times now, but Jack would have been consumed with it back then with me behind the wheel. As it was, he was so angry one night, he literally drove the car into the side of a moving train. He was determined he had the right of way as he tried to beat the train before the crossing gate came down. I was terrified and screaming. The train was travelling slowly and stopped. I don't know how Jack escaped charges. Sometimes I had to shake myself to remind me all that was in the past.

Ben, on the other hand, was a patient instructor. Thanks to his careful instruction, I'm still driving in my 80's and I'm still behind the wheel of a Cadillac. I've never driven anything else because I feel so safe in these solid cars. In Kamloops, the Caddy told everyone that I was a successful businesswoman. I'll admit, also, that it added a bit of glamour, too. I still feel that way. And, I'm a good driver. You'll never find this woman slowing traffic in the fast lane!

Our trip home that October took us back into Canada and then down through New York State to the Adirondacs and into New England just as the late fall colours were at their most glorious. After stopping in Augusta, the capital of Maine, we visited friends before the last lap of our journey home to Presque Isle. It was good to be back.

Sometimes Ted would catch me looking at him and he'd say, "What is it, Hon?" I'd be thinking how much I loved everything about him. He was a good dresser, always well groomed. He was tall, over six feet, with blue eyes, a cleft in his chin and a warm smile. His hair was dark and wavy. He had what he called "the pharmacist's slouch" from always bending over the counter. I've never seen a man with such long, slender fingers and, as for his voice, I'd know it anywhere. Even after all these years I remember everything as if it were yesterday.

I learned, too, that he had a very compassionate nature. His father was a pharmacist and left the business to Ted, his eldest son. Ted knew that some of his customers couldn't pay for prescriptions. "How can you say no to a sick parent?" he would say to me. Presque Isle was a small enough community that no one was anonymous. Like the teachers and doctors, Ted knew which families needed a helping hand when times were tough.

Ted was also appreciative and encouraging. All my nesting instincts, making a comfortable home, preparing good meals, soft lights and music at the end of the day—he noticed every detail. While we were away he said to me, "I don't have a good enough home for you, Margaret." His life had been such a mess, he said. He only stayed home long enough to sleep and left again to go back to the store before he finally left his house to his wife and moved in with his mother.

"I had to leave it behind, Margaret," he told me, "to make a fresh start. It had too many bad memories."

"We'll make a home, together," I reassured him.

And now, we returned to the serious business of finding a house that would become our home. When we set our minds to it, we found one. The owners were moving to California so we were able to move in for our first Christmas together. Our new house had two bedrooms and two bathrooms, a living and dining room together, my sewing room, a kitchen of course and a large 'rumpus' room in a finished basement. Rumpus rooms were all the rage back in the fifties, before family rooms became the fashion. We had both ping-pong and billiard tables down there. I wanted it to be a fun place for my new family.

One day, Ted surprised me with a dachshund puppy, Hans. He knew how hard it had been to leave my little Fritz back at the Mayfair. It didn't take long before Hans was one of the family, always running to the door, barking excitedly, when he heard Ted drive into the garage at the end of the day.

"You'll have a hard time trying to match that welcome," Ted would laugh. I always did better than that.

It seemed we were hardly settled in before we were

Our first home.

Our dog Hans.

off again on another trip south. This time we stopped along the way to meet more of Ted's family in Connecticut and New York City and we went dancing at the famous Rainbow Room. I remembered my last trip to New York, when Joe showed me around the town. New York felt familiar and comfortable but I must admit I still had to look up at the skyscrapers! And when I did, I thought of Gordon.

Driving down the East Coast, we stopped in Washington, DC before, at last, finding our way back to the Mirador—the place where Ted and I met, just two whirlwind years ago.

Ted made travelling fun. Every morning I fixed breakfast in the room where we had a hot plate and a coffee maker. Half a freshly picked grapefruit, corn flakes and sometimes a poached egg and we were ready for the road. I often packed sandwiches, which we ate, picnic style at a rest stop along the way. By late in the afternoon, before darkness set in, we found a motel and settled in. A good dinner at night ended a perfect day. Ted was always so appreciative of everything I did to make the trip comfortable, it just made me want to do more for him.

Of course, I look at motels and hotels from an insider's point of view. When I first step into a room I look for a comfortable bed, two good pillows, extra blankets and a good bedside reading light. I've always liked to read in bed and a good light is essential. I don't want to have to get out of bed to turn it off, either. A phone in the room and an icemaker not too far away are important, also. These are the little touches that don't cost that much but make a real difference toward making a stay pleasant.

People often told me how much they appreciated the flowers and books I provided at the Mayfair. I had the best beds, good pillows, two extra, and big thirsty towels. As the owner operator I wanted to know what people thought about my place. And I was successful.

To this day, I like to make houseguests feel pampered and comfortable. Good pillows, an extra blanket, a bedside lamp and some good books and magazines, hangers in the closet, and flowers tell friends and relatives they are special. And one more thing—a comfortable chair!

We loved being back in Florida. The memory of those painful jellyfish welts kept me from the ocean but we swam in the motel pool and played golf every day. Ted had a romantic and impetuous side to him and one morning, while reading the paper and sipping his first coffee of the day, he asked, "What would you say to a Caribbean cruise, Mrs. Thompson?"

In a few days, our names were listed on a cruise ship bound for fourteen days of Caribbean island hopping. As a matter of fact, it was one of the last passenger lists produced on any cruise ship. Evidently, so many couples were travelling with someone other than their spouses, the lists were considered indiscreet and the practice ended!

Having fun on the ship.

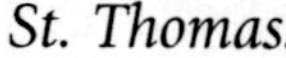
St. Thomas.

Curaçao.

On the day we landed in Venezuela we took a train through a tunnel in mountains to Caracas. It was a beautiful colonial Spanish city. After lunching beside the pool at the Hotel Tamanaco, we continued our tour of the city. I was appalled at the poverty, which surrounded one of the most luxurious hotels in South America. It was probably the first time I understood that, although Betty and I considered ourselves poor after Father died; we were very fortunate. Looking at the little children on the streets of Caracas, I wondered what they would have to do to get enough to eat, let alone to have a warm bath and clean clothes to replace the rags they wore. They wore shoes made out of rubber tires and lived in hovels.

Swimming pool on freighter.

Hotel Tamanaco.

It seemed such a contrast back aboard the ship as we continued our cruise. We were seated at the captain's table. He was an Italian. A crewmember told us he met with very few people on his cruises as a rule. The reason we were at his table was that our travel agent thought we would be interesting table mates and mentioned us to him. Ted could understand a little Italian and he and the captain shared an interest in coins and stamps. He had a very good sense of humour. A French couple and two other women joined us; a bank president's wife, and the wife of an aircraft manufacturer. Ted could talk to anyone and I enjoyed meeting new people, too.

Along the way, standing at the ship's rail, I could spend hours gazing at the ocean, imagining what lay beyond the horizon. Our stops included the French island of Martinique where the statue of Josephine Bonaparte stands in the harbour and where, sitting on the quay, we spotted schools of tiny silver fish jumping out of the water in fan formation. In Santo Domingo, we arrived just in time for the Latin American fair. It was the first time I saw naked girls dancing. They wore massive head dresses, long white gloves and strategically placed little white powder puffs.

One day the captain invited us to the bridge so we could watch the ship sail into San Juan, Puerto Rico. A pilot came aboard to navigate the huge vessel into port. Our captain suddenly became extremely agitated. "You are bringing her in far too fast," he shouted, and pushing the pilot aside, he grabbed the wheel and shoved the ship into reverse. It was too late. We rammed the dock with a mighty wallop. I don't know what the folks below deck thought or if anyone was hurt. I was glad that both Ted and I were not thrown off our feet.

"They don't know my ship," our captain told us.

Our last stop was Havana. In 1956, before Castro overthrew the dictator, Battista, Havana was another beautiful colonial city. A graveyard, just like a city, with a tomb of Italian marble from Carrara was, to our eyes, a strange sight.

As we headed home, Ted and I both agreed we were hooked on cruising. I loved the shipboard life and so did Ted.

We drove through the Everglades on our way through Florida where we saw the Seminole Indians fishing, sitting high in the back of airboats. We stayed with our friends, the Boutelles. Besides a beautiful home, they had three guesthouses on their beautiful beachfront property. Mr. Boutelle was quite a character. Before his daily swim off the beach, he always drank a large vodka and orange juice.

We also visited friends we met on board the ship. Ted often picked up the tab for the single women seated at our table and this particular lady invited us to her home, I suppose to return his hospitality. We were enchanted with her white colonial mansion and garden, which was blooming with azaleas of many colours. With lots of servants, she and her husband lived a very gracious life. I was uncomfortable, though, when a black man came to carry our suitcases. He seemed far too old to be lifting our bags. Ted said it was expected.

Up through the Blue Ridge Mountains, dogwood and many other trees were blossoming. Fresh green leaves waking up all around us. It was good to be alive. We stopped at the historical village of Williamsburg, experiencing life as the colonists did over two hundred years ago, and then drove on to Washington and the Smithsonian. If I was going to live in the U.S., there was no time like now to learn more about the country's history and achievement. James Smithson founded The Smithsonian Institution in 1842. He established the national museum for the increase and discussion of knowledge. Our visit was only long enough to see the Hope Diamond and some of the early airplanes. I told Ted we would have to pay a return visit. "Only if you take me as your guide," he responded.

One last stop to stay with Ted's sister and her husband—more family to meet! I liked them instantly. We took the Staten Island ferry, the one they always show in romantic movies with New York as a backdrop. After that visit we would drive down and stay with them often, to see a play or visit art galleries and the Metropolitan Museum.

Back in Maine, spring was in the air. In May, the potato farmers started to get the fields ready for planting.

The potato fields in bloom are quite a sight. In the fall, if the first frost doesn't kill the tops, the farmers spray them with a herbicide. Then, the children are excused from school to help harvest the crop. They separate the rocks from the potatoes, throwing the rocks aside, filling baskets with potatoes and then dumping the baskets into big barrels, as trucks go up and down the rows. At that time, most of the crop was grown for seed potatoes and ended up in cold storage for the winter.

To see children helping their parents during the harvest is not unusual in many parts of the world but I was surprised to see this in Maine. I also thought about the poor children I saw in the Caribbean. Farm children, at least, have food on their plates at the end of the day. I remembered how we helped father cut the gypsum and work in the garden. We knew that he needed our help and we never thought of ourselves as child labourers. And then, after he died and Jack was wasting away whatever money we might have had, Betty and I just had to go to work. Nobody seemed surprised when I left school to do housework for Mrs. Archibald. In New Westminster, in the 1930s, many students, but particularly, many girls, did not finish high school. When I became aware of the terrible conditions in which many of the world's children lived, I thought, how lucky we were. We were not afraid of hard work thanks to father and mother's good teaching.

Settling back into a comfortable routine in our new home, I began to learn about the drug store business. In the fall, Ted always had a 'two-for-one' sale and I was soon helping him with that. As I also took my turn at the soda fountain, making banana splits with chocolate, strawberry and vanilla ice cream, topped with nuts, whipped cream and a cherry, or double malted chocolate milkshakes, I realized how much I missed the people coming and going at the Mayfair. This was fun. In that small town, everyone came into the drug store to visit and this was a way for the community to meet Ted's new wife.

One day a little boy came into the store to buy some penny candy Ted always had on the counter. He was very disappointed to be told he didn't have enough money for the candy he wanted. Disgustedly, he put his coins on the counter and left, saying, "Keep it. It won't buy anything, anyway!"

Before long, it was Christmas. It was such fun buying gifts for my new family, decorating the house, and planning dinner for twenty-two!

From then on, after Christmas Ted and I left Maine's cold winter for a break in sunny Florida. In 1957, we cut short our stay there to attend the Rotary International Convention in Switzerland. It was my first trip to Europe and Ted, always generous, said, "After the convention, I'd love to show you some more of Europe." I couldn't wait. I never thought I'd be travelling to Europe.

Chapter 7

Europe

Early in April, we were off! From Gander, in Newfoundland, we flew to Munich and then travelled by train to Switzerland. Our plane fare was $860 return. It was a lot in those days, but for Ted, it was the trip of a lifetime. Later, when I made quite a bit of money from the sale of the motel I paid my share of our travels. I was used to being financially independent and always say that every woman should have money of her own.

"Mad money," Mrs. Archibald called it. "You always have it so you can go home from a party if you want to." There was no way I wanted to leave the party. Ted and I were having too much fun. Even so, I liked to have a little financial independence.

I was proud to be Canadian when, on the plane across the Atlantic, some Americans on board said our Rockies were just as beautiful as the Swiss Alps. I would soon be able to see for myself.

In Lucerne, we stayed in a charming old house owned by a lovely elderly couple. We could see the lake from the top of our street. A beautiful eiderdown comforter kept us warm on the cool spring nights. We ate our meals at our own table in the dining room where each place had a little cloth envelope where you put your serviette for the next meal. Our hosts would do anything for us, including sewing a button on Ted's coat and mending a seam in my nightgown.

Lucerne is a beautiful city. One night the Rotarians set adrift thousands of lighted candles on the lake from which the city takes its name. The candlelight reflected in the lake under a starry sky was a sight I'll never forget.

Because most of the other couples registered at the conference were staying outside Lucerne, they brought their evening clothes to our place so they could change without having to leave the city to dress and then come all the way back for the evening events. One night we all hired a limousine and eight of us drove up to a beautiful old hotel in the mountains. After a wonderful dinner, followed by dancing a good part of the night away, we returned to our hotel only to find the door locked tight. We roused the owner, who, dressed in a long nightshirt and bed cap, came grumpily down to open the door and let us in. A short while after our friends left, we heard pebbles rattling against our window. Looking down, we saw our friends. They had forgotten some of their things under our bed. We needed a key to open the door, so, once again, apologetically, we wakened our, by this time, even grumpier host. Once again he trundled down and let them in. A little while later, we couldn't believe our ears. There were more pebbles. Our friends, for the third time, were beneath our window. This time we threw the things down to them. In the morning, not a word was said when we entered the dining room. Our hosts were as pleasant as ever.

After the convention we set out on a grand tour of Europe by bus conducted by Rotary International. From Basel we sailed down the Rhine past the beautiful old castles and vineyards along the banks. In Heidelberg we danced on top of the largest beer barrel in the world to the music of a German 'oompa' band. After Ted won at blackjack in the casino at Wiesbaden, our guide suggested he quit while he was ahead, so we cashed in his chips and bought the Dresden figurines that sit in my glass fronted cabinet today.

Although it was now twelve years after the Second World War, we saw much damage still evident in Germany. The rebuilding of the beautiful Cologne Cathedral was still in progress. I was glad our trip to Hitler's hide away, far up in the Bavarian mountains was brief. I must admit, it gave me the willies just to think that a few short years ago one of the most evil men in history once stood in that very same spot.

When our tour bus stopped at the Allied cemetery at Dunkirk, many of our companions walked sadly among the crosses, locating relatives buried there. Row upon row of crosses brought the reality of what the war had meant in terms of human loss. Our coach was very quiet as we drove off.

As the bus took us through the Netherlands, I thought we couldn't have chosen a better time to visit. Miles and miles of bright tulip and daffodil fields were in bloom. Wherever we went, Ted brought fresh flowers to our hotel room. He was so generous. If I ever wanted something but felt it was too costly, he would say, "Go ahead and buy it. We can afford it." Something held me back. Whether it was growing up poor or having to work hard for my money initially, I was cautious about spending too much in those days.

Recently I read a marvellous love story, *Tulip Fever.* Set in the Netherlands, it is the story of a young woman married to a much older burgher. Her husband hires a young artist to paint her and, of course, the artist and the young wife fall in love. Tulip fever refers to a period back in the 1700's when the Dutch began speculating wildly in tulip bulbs. This gambling led to vast sums of money being borrowed and, alas, lost when the market fell. It reminded me of the time when my father said the market had fallen back in the twenties. Market speculation, which ruined so many people in the Depression, has a long history.

In Amsterdam we boarded a canal boat for sightseeing and unexpectedly saw rats. A guide told us there were twice as many rats as people in Amsterdam.

Our next stop was Copenhagen. That night we all went to the Tivoli Gardens. Its millions of lights reminded me of the candles on Lake Lucerne. It was a fairyland.

In Stockholm we toured a hospital so large that the nurses went from ward to ward on bicycles. And then we arrived in Helsinki. Our hotel was right on the harbour. In spite of a wonderful market filled with all kinds of fish and fresh vegetables and the busyness of the city, Helsinki and the Finns seemed very sombre. It was chilling to see Russian soldiers parade in the streets and sobering to visit another cemetery, this time of Russian war dead. Once again, grave markers as far as the eye could see. Nearby was a great wall inscribed with thousands of names; those of Finns killed in the Second World War.

Our tour took us over to Norway where we saw Edvard Grieg's home and a famous Norwegian stave church before sailing up the Trondheim Fjord. Our guided trip ended with a choppy boat ride across the North Sea, and a bus ride to Edinburgh. We said goodbye to our friends, and set off on our own by car to see Scotland and to play some golf on its world famous courses.

If anyone had told me, when we were playing golf on that course the boys made back in Kamloops, the ones with tomato cans for the holes and the sandy 'greens', that I would one day find myself teeing off at St. Andrews, I would have said, "You're dreaming!" And yet, here we were, ready to tee off the next morning, after arriving late the night before from Gleneagles. There was just one problem. As I lay in bed beside a sleepy Ted, I could hear the rain. It was pouring buckets. There would be no golf for us that day.

The rain had stopped by the next morning, but high winds were the price of a cloudless sky. I said, "We haven't come all this way to be put off by a windy day. Let's have breakfast and get started. It will feel great to stretch our legs and get some exercise." And, it did! Breakfast was eggs, rashers of streaky bacon, scones, and fried tomatoes. We had read about St. Andrews. It was right on the ocean and challenging. By this time, I had a respectable drive, not long but straight, and my chip shots were pretty good, too.

I mentally thanked Mrs. Brinkworth, the pro's wife in Jasper, who taught me all I knew about golfing etiquette. If ever there was a time for good manners, this was it. At that time, many women just followed their husbands from tee to tee. Not me, I was just as eager as Ted to test my golf game on this famous course. It was the opportunity of a lifetime. Our caddie was a young Scots lad.

Ted always enjoyed a scotch before dinner. There in St. Andrews, we sampled some of the best single malt available, smoky and peatty, sitting in front of a window looking over a panorama of hills of heather and a blue sky turning to red as evening descended. It was heaven.

Healthily tired after our day on the course, we had dinner in our hotel and settled for an early bed.

The next day we were heading north to Dundee and then on to Balmoral to see the Queen!

Like most Canadians, I always had a healthy interest in the 'Royals'. I admired the Queen's pluckiness during the Second World War, felt sympathy for 'Bertie', the Duke of York catapulted into public view by his brother's affair with 'that woman', Wallis Simpson. I followed the little princesses as they grew up. I knew Balmoral was the holiday estate Elizabeth and Phillip loved; the place where they could relax, do some fishing and join in some Scottish country dancing with their friends and neighbours in the evenings. As the Queen was in residence, her standard flying high above the huge mansion, we couldn't enter the estate. Although disappointed, I was delighted with the rhododendrons all around us. They were in full bloom and magnificent, in all colours. My love affair with rhododendrons began that day. I have several varieties in my garden, now. These hardy and beautiful plants grow well on both the east and west coasts.

As we drove through the lowlands, along the creeks and burns, Ted and I discovered restaurants were few and far between. We'd heard about pub lunches but not many pubs were in evidence. Sometimes we bought a picnic lunch from the vans that travelled the country roads. Cheese buns, classic Scottish shortbread and fruit, with fresh water to wash it down, made an ample feast at the side of the road on those lovely spring days.

We headed out west from Aberdeen to Inverness and then into the Highlands. Ted was driving and we got lost. Suddenly we were on the wrong side of the road. "I think we'd better pull over and look at a map," I said, laughing, glad there was no traffic.

"I think you're right," he agreed. I couldn't help thinking how different things had been with Jack behind the wheel. I wouldn't have dared question his driving or his judgment. Jack would have been cursing and in a foul mood for the rest of the day. Things were so easy with Ted. He told me sometimes he too thought about the way things had been with his first wife. It wasn't as if we were a couple of kids who just left the past behind us, either. We both had regrets about how things had turned out in our first marriages but we were both so grateful that we had found each other.

My stepmother was a romantic. She told us about Bonnie Prince Charlie leaving his true love, Flora MacDonald, behind on the Isle of Skye when he was exiled from his homeland. I told Ted I just had to see the island, so we took the boat over. All the way across I could hear my stepmother singing the old ballad, *Speed Bonny Boat.*

Back on the mainland, we played another round of golf at Tunberry, where, during the war, the hotel had housed the military and the course was used as a landing field. That night we danced at the hotel with some of the locals. At last, I thought, we'll be dancing the jigs and reels and elegant strathspeys of traditional Scottish country dancing. Not a chance! There were a lot of American tourists and we ended up in a conga line! I was wearing a strapless yellow dress which was just right in that setting.

Our Scottish journey ended back in Edinburgh, just in time to hear the skirl of the pipes at the famous Edinburgh Tattoo, with massed bands from all over the Commonwealth. It was a sight to behold.

Father often told us about William Wordsworth, how he lived in the Lake District and what an energetic walker he was. Both our parents could recite long passages from poems and plays. "I wandered lonely as a cloud," they would begin. My brother Jack's eyes would roll, but mother and father would be off and there was no stopping them.

"One day," father often told us, "I'll take you all to see his house and we will follow in his footsteps through the Lake District." He never stopped looking for a rabbit every morning, the rabbit who would change his fortune and make it possible for him to take us back to his homeland, to see all the ancient sites and the places we knew only through our history books. His fortunes changed all right, but not for the better.

But here I was, looking down from Hadrian's Wall, joining the shoppers on Princess Street in Edinburgh, playing golf at St. Andrews and now driving towards the Cumbrian Mountains. We would soon be following Wordsworth's path. Would we see his 'host of golden daffodils'?

As we drove south toward the Lake District, I remembered father telling us of his walks in the Cumbrian hills. I said to Ted, as we neared Ambleside and Derwentwater, "Let's stop and walk a bit." He agreed.

The sky was blue with just a 'lonely cloud' or two. Behind the stone fences, sheep grazed contentedly, taking no notice of us at all. The daffodils were everywhere. "If only father was here," I thought.

We left the Lake District behind and drove on to Stratford on Avon to see *Romeo and Juliet*, and to Oxford with its ancient spires and many colleges. I told Ted, once again, standing inside the Sheldonian Theatre, my only regret about my life so far was that I had not completed my education. "Remember what I've told you. You got your education in the university of life, sweetheart," he smiled. "You may not have a formal education, but you are not ignorant. You are looking, listening and learning new things all the time." Ted never made me feel inferior.

We stopped in London just long enough to check on our flight home in ten days by way of Paris, and to drop the car off. Ted said, "I've had enough of driving." To tell the truth, I was relieved when he said that. Those narrow country lanes and roundabouts in the towns were hair-raising. Being able to stop for tea when we found a lovely country inn and not being restricted by a tight schedule, gave us a very personal view of England and Scotland. What lovely memories we would take home with us. I was just as glad, now though, to let someone else do the driving.

I could hardly wait for the last leg of our journey. "We'll be having scones with strawberry jam and clotted cream with our tea," I told Ted.

"First stop the ancient and mysterious stone circles at Stonehenge and Salisbury Cathedral not to mention Bath," he reminded me. "I told you before we left, I'll show you everything." Touring the West Country and Tintagel, haunted by the legends of King Arthur, then Devon, Dartmoor, Penzance and along the rugged coast to Plymouth, in a few short days we returned to London.

Although Ted had planned an itinerary for our trip, we sometimes had surprises and changed our plans to suit. The weather had been perfect. The last rainy day was at Saint Andrews. We looked forward with great excitement to see a tennis match at Wimbledon. Ted arranged for tickets right at centre court. This was England. It rained. We had our strawberries and cream undercover and then went back to watch the men's final. Then to Ascot. We bet on the horses and I wore a smart navy and white suit with a matching hat, and I felt a little like Eliza Dolittle as Ted placed our bets. "I wonder if anyone here guesses that I came up the hard way, a little girl from New Westminster." Luckily, I wasn't serious and had learned to laugh at myself.

The next morning Ted was one of the speakers at a Rotarian meeting. He left me having a leisurely breakfast in our room, enjoying the view from the Dorchester Hotel, which overlooked Regent's Park. After the meeting,

Ted called me excitedly from the hotel lobby. "Get down here right away! We're going to see Queen Elizabeth christen the *Cutty Sark* !" One of the other speakers was an inspector from Scotland Yard. He and Ted were chatting after the meeting and he suggested the surprise. I was downstairs within minutes and we were soon aboard the police boat. On the trip down the Thames to Greenwich, while the crew served us tea and scones, the inspector pointed out some of the sights and showed us the place where, in the old days, they used to tie prisoners to the quays at low tide. They died a slow death when the river rose at high tide.

We knew it was unlikely that we would see the Queen at Balmoral so we weren't disappointed when the only view was of those magnificent rhododendrons. Now it was almost our last day in England and here we were watching her as she broke the traditional bottle of champagne over the bow of the beautiful sailing craft. I was so excited I left my camera behind on the police boat. Ted assured me, "Don't worry. It couldn't possibly be in better hands."

Sure enough, the police returned it to us the next day just before we left for Paris.

Never mind Paris in springtime, Paris in June is fabulous! Everything they say about Paris is true. Every movie I'd ever seen about Paris, from *Singing in the Rain* with Gene Kelly, Audrey Hepburn in *Sabrina* and *Love in the Afternoon,* Maurice Chevalier and Leslie Caron dancing and singing in *Gigi*, it's all true! The Champs Elysee, the Eiffel Tower and the Louvre. At the Louvre my feet finally said, "Enough!" I walked in bliss, carrying my shoes. The Mona Lisa was such a surprise. In my mind the picture was large. It was, in fact, a small painting of the woman with the secret smile. We had dinner at Maxim's and saw the Aga Khan's name on the guest list, right above our names. We were shocked soon after to read the headlines in all the papers. The Aga Khan was dead.

The next night we went night clubbing, drinking champagne at the Follies Bergeres and the Lido. And then on our last day in the 'City of Lights', Ted had tickets for the Fourth of July celebration at the American Embassy. I had no idea there were so many Americans in Paris. The party was so crowded, we didn't stay long. Ted had one remaining treat for me, lunch at La Tour D'Argent. After we ordered the spéciaité de la maison, pressed duck, the waiter presented the bird for our approval. While we waited for the chef to cook the duck, I'm afraid we drank too much wine. No regrets, though. Is good French wine as wonderful as they say it is? Mais oui!

At last we were on our way home. We had seen and done everything. Ted kept saying. "We don't know if we'll ever do this again. I want to show you everything." He had.

Chapter 8

Farewell to the Mayfair

Betty and her son Keath were coming to stay in a few short days. I had so much to do before they arrived.

While we were touring Europe, our wonderful cleaning lady, Hazel Cyr, stayed at the house. She lived in Portage Lake and so enjoyed staying in town while we were away. A few weeks in town gave her the opportunity to visit with family and friends. She unpacked, washed and ironed all my clothes so I was able to catch up on the gardening chores. Hazel was a jewel, just like Dorothy and Janet back in Kamloops, people who could do what needed doing without having every detail spelled out for them. I always find that, if you trust people to do good work for you, if you let them go to work with a minimum of interference, if you pay them decently and praise them for a job well done, your staff will always rise to the challenge.

I hadn't seen Betty for two years. We took Keath to a resort on the coast, where he could canoe while Betty and I caught up on everything that had happened to each of us. I wanted to know if Betty was happy with Art, and of course, she wanted to know all about my new life with Ted. It was good to have the freedom to go to bed late, if we felt like talking all night. In the years since my marriage to Jack, I never had a friend who took the place of Betty. We had been so close when we were growing up. Of course we talked on the phone, but it wasn't the same as being right there. I was sorry to see her go back to the other side of the continent.

Ted and I did a lot of travelling. We drove down to Georgia and also returned every year to Hollywood Beach in Florida. In 1959, we drove back to Maine in the spring to learn that Uncle Ben had been injured. Since my marriage to Ted, Ben had been managing the motor court. He prided himself on his handyman skills and when anything broke down, he always tried to fix it himself. He was up on the roof, cleaning and unplugging a downspout, when he slipped and fell to the ground. I was worried about him so Ted and I decided to head back to Kamloops.

We were in the middle of packing our bags when Ted received a summons to appear in court. Jack, living in Victoria now, wanted to remarry and decided that he wanted a divorce. He named Ted as the correspondent. From here in 2002, looking back to the fifties, the divorce process in those days seems very sordid. As I mentioned before, back then, the only way you could get a divorce in Canada was to prove your partner was an adulterer. Private detectives made a good living from catching couples in the act. I'm not one of those seniors who thinks everything in the old days was better. Some things are much better now.

Ted and I set off across the continent. We took our time, stopping to see the Grand Tetons, Yellowstone, Waterton, and Banff National Parks. We also played golf at Jasper, the course where I learned to play. The starter took exception to my white shorts and sent me back for a skirt.

When we finally arrived in Kamloops, Janet and Dorothy welcomed us with relief. Ben had not recovered from his head injury and managing the Mayfair was just too much for them all. They had all done their best to keep the business going, but I could see that it was not fair to leave them with all the responsibility. I think I always knew that to manage a small business successfully, you have to be right there all the time. Ask any franchiser and you will discover that even a franchise is only as good as the on-site manager. And that means many hours on site.

There were more than a few tears amongst us all when I said I had decided to sell the business. For Ben, the Mayfair was his home as well as an investment. For Dorothy, hard work at the court was a refuge from the grief she would always carry for her son, Les. For Janet, it was a time to move on. Ben continued to be part of the family, spending six months with us in Maine, and six months with Betty and Art in New Westminster. As for me, I knew my home was now in Maine, with Ted.

But first, it was time to pick up that hammer again. And the scrub and the paint brushes, as well. All of us worked like the proverbial Canadian beaver, repairing windows, replacing light bulbs, painting and polishing. Then it was out in the garden, where we weeded, trimmed the lawns, pruned the shrubs, dug in the compost and planted primroses, marigolds and the geraniums that Uncle Ben always started from cuttings near the end of winter.

I needed advice about selling the Mayfair. I did some research and discovered there was a real estate firm that dealt exclusively in selling auto courts. I listed the motel with them and several weeks later, a young Japanese businessman offered my asking price. He had the down payment I wanted and I carried the 6% mortgage. He also agreed to make twice-yearly payments on the principle.

While we were in Kamloops, Ted received a second summons. Davie Fulton handled everything for us, once again. Jack got his divorce but, because I had paid him his share of the Mayfair a few years before, he didn't receive another red cent from me. I hadn't seen him for years. Sometimes I wonder what became of him. I hope he never remarried, but if he did, I pity his poor wife. There were no shelters for battered women in those days. Abuse was kept behind closed doors.

The divorce and the sale of the auto court marked the end of my old life. Like Janet, Dorothy and Ben, I was sad to leave that life behind but knew there was a whole new world out there for Ted and me to explore.

Chapter 9

On the Road

Ted and I discovered a mutual love of travelling early in our relationship. Ted, though, protested that on our first trip across the continent with Uncle Ben, he was pursuing me, and not new places. "I didn't want to let you out of my sight, hon," he said.

Over the years, as well, I always cherished that happy memory of our family road trip, when we left Invermere for New Westminster. That was such a happy, carefree time for us.

Back in Maine, it was not very long before we were on a road trip across the country again. In the fifties, everyone with a car and some extra cash, hit the road.

"Let's hop in the car and drive to California," was a common refrain then on the west coast. Mom, Dad, grandma and the kids piled in the family car and were off, down through Washington and Oregon, to California to see how the stars lived in Hollywood, enjoy the new spectacular attraction in Los Angeles, Disneyland, and then continue down the road to the San Diego Zoo and finally, exotic if dismal Tijuana. Back then, as hard as it is to believe now, the Canadian dollar was worth more than the American. Along the way, there were plenty of drive-in restaurants with car hops eager to bring your meals right to the car on long trays which stretched across the front and back seats from window to window. Down the highway south of Bellingham, there was a even a roadside restaurant in the shape of an orange. Every kid wanted to stop there for a treat. I discovered it was just the same in Maine. Almost everyone hit the road, heading south, stopping at the drive-ins, and staying at the auto courts. I now know that I entered the motel business at just the right time. I also felt confident that if I ever had to earn my living again, provided I had the initial capital, I could do it.

Before I left B.C. behind me, we agreed to meet Betty and Arthur in Palm Desert. For them, it was a short drive down the coast. For us, it meant another cross country marathon, down through West Virginia, Tennessee, Arkansas and Texas before the final leg of the trip, across New Mexico and Arizona.

There's nothing I like better than getting behind the wheel of a good, solid car. I still love it. Ted did most of the driving, while I was the navigator. I have no trouble reading maps and if I need help, I don't mind asking.

I made breakfast in our unit early each morning. We both had our coffee and orange juice and then, while Ted found a morning paper, I boiled eggs and made toast.

Over the years, I filled my address book with names and addresses of folks who stayed at the Mayfair. And, of course we often made friends with people on cruises or tours. All of us have said at one time or another, "Do get in touch if your ever in town", while exchanging addresses and phone numbers or sending cards at Christmas time. Sometimes, indeed, we do find ourselves in town, making that phone call that ends in a visit. Only once, did this prove to be trouble, but more about that later. I often visited with such friends while Ted made a point of connecting with fellow Rotarians wherever we went. This also gave us each a little time away from each other.

Often on our road trips, I thought of those old National Geographics at home—the ones with the blue Caddy on the back. I often got the latest issue and lay on my tummy on the floor, pouring over the pictures, dreaming of one day travelling to the far off places described in the articles. Even so, I'd never heard of some of the places Ted and I visited now. Ted was always indulgent when it came to stopping along the way, but usually, in the morning, while he read the paper, I'd look at the map and read the guidebooks for the area.

This trip took us into Utah, through the Canyon Lands National Park and Archer's National Park. We visited the Carlsbad caverns. We were amazed at the stalactites, a deposit of calcium carbonate resembling icicles hanging from the roof of the caves, and the stalagmites rising from the floor, in all shapes and sizes.

When we emerged from the caves, I was relieved to breathe fresh air once again.

I guess one thing never changed for me, since I was a toddler back in Invermere. I still love wildflowers and I still want to stop the car to gather bunches of them. On that trip I remember the blue bonnets blooming in Texas.

Although we always checked the weather ahead on our portable radio, on this trip we were caught in a sandstorm in Texas. The air was so thick with sand that we had to pull off the road.

It was terrifying. Usually, if the weather showed signs of closing in, we'd stay put. We had the luxury of time when we were on the road.

When we finally met Betty and Art in Palm Desert, we were tired of the road and ready for some serious relaxation. That meant golf, of course and some side trips when we felt rested again.

One day a group of us decided to catch the train down to Mazatlan and while we waited at the station, Art's suitcase disappeared. He lost his good clothes and a shaving kit and we all learned to keep our eyes on our belongings.

On our way back east, Ted and I stopped in Las Vegas. There was something about the fellow who checked us into our hotel that made me uneasy. That night, after taking in some of the shows, we were tired and went to bed without putting the safety chain on our door.

I woke in the night, thinking I heard someone in the room. I sat up in bed and listened. Nothing. So, I went back to sleep, sure that I was imagining things and not wanting to disturb Ted. In the morning, Ted realized right away that his money clip was gone, and with it, all his cash.

We called the police, but we knew there wasn't much they could do. "Keep your cash under your pillow, from now on," they advised. Fortunately, I had some money in my evening bag, but we would need to get some more before very long.

Continuing on our way home, we stopped in Cortez, Colorado, where we stayed at a lovely wayside inn which served family style meals. Some other tourists from New York invited us to go down to a nearby Hopi reservation. The Hopi invited us into their hogans, showing us some rock paintings and beautiful weaving, done with the wool from their own sheep herds. A winding, narrow road, with a sheer drop in many places of several hundred feet with no guard rail, took us to the Mesa Verde Plateau, where the Ansazi natives once lived in cliff dwellings. It was like stepping back into time, eerie, because the homes had long since been empty. It was easy to imagine the ghosts of those former times, living freely in that beautiful country and before the native peoples and their culture were displaced by the coming of European settlers.

We were running short of money. The cash in my evening bag was almost gone and Ted was left with change only. Few people had credit cards back in those days and it was hard to get money from a bank in a town where nobody knew you. I suggested that Ted contact a fellow Rotarian, and he would have done that but we were near to Colorado Springs, where some friends of his mother's lived.

We found their home, knocked on their door and prayed they were at home. They were and they went with Ted, to vouch for him at the bank. We thanked them and headed for Denver, the mile high city, home of the US Air Force Academy. We drove through Kansas and Missouri, stopped in St. Louis with its huge welcoming arch, and still on Highway 70, we passed through Illinois, Indiana and Ohio, finally, reaching New York. We made a beeline for home. 'Home'. How easy it was to make the transition from the West to the East Coast. How right 'home' felt to us both.

Home. The first time Ted came out to the Cariboo country he said, "Margaret, I can't wait to see the cottage at Paul Lake you are always talking about." He knew that leaving the cabin behind was difficult for me. It was my refuge when, after the busy tourist season was over, I needed a break from the unrelenting work at the Mayfair. It was also the one place I could count on Jack behaving himself. Everyone was on their best behaviour there, and no one ever needed a second invitation to "Come out to the lake, this weekend."

I didn't want to tell Ted how much I missed my little get-away, but one evening, after dinner, he said, "You know, hon, I've been thinking about that cottage of yours again. What would you say to us building a cabin up at Portage Lake?"

Chapter 10

Mayfair Cottage at Portage Lake

That was Ted. He could almost read my mind. Once we decided to go ahead, we moved quickly. We bought a lot, found a builder, and soon we had a lovely cottage. Although I didn't take up a hammer this time, I spent many contended hours at the sewing machine, making curtains and bedspreads. "Thanks, dear Mrs. Archibald," I said, "For teaching me sewing skills."

One of the camp's nicest features was the field stone fireplace, always burning if there was a chill in the air. Braided rugs, knotty pine panelling and furniture we bought in Boston made it feel like another world although it was just 35 miles from town.

We were there almost every weekend, along with an assortment of Ted's children and grandchildren, as well as friends. We bought a canoe for quiet times on the water and a power boat for water skiing. It was Ted's idea to call our hideaway, 'Mayfair' and we had a big open house or camp warming when it was finished. Uncle Ben, one of our first guests, stayed with us to celebrate Thanksgiving.

Cottage near Presque Isle.

Grandchildren visiting.

In January, I decided to take a run out to the camp to check on things and stayed the night, after warming up the cottage. I awoke the next morning to eight inches of snow. It was so quiet and so beautiful and I had time to reflect that we needed to be alone there, sometimes. It's the way I feel in my garden now, a need to be silent, to listen, to hear the grass growing, as my father used to say. "You know, Margaret," he often said, "If you want to be a successful landscaper, you must observe the landscape. Pay attention to how your plants are growing in each part of the garden. They will tell you, 'We like it here,' or 'This is too shady for us, here.'" It's true! I grow prize-winning fuchsias and beautiful roses in my garden. When people ask me my secret for success, I tell them what fertilizers I use but I also say, "Stand still in your garden in the early morning or just before dusk, and look and listen to what your plants are telling you. Maybe conditions are not right in your garden for fuscias. If not, plant dahlias or geraniums." It's always a good idea to join your local garden club, as well. Nobody can give you as good advice as another gardener.

Dock on shore for winter.

I still have the guest book we kept at the cottage from those golden days. Looking back to 1965, I see the year was filled with guests, including one couple who even spent their honeymoon there in the dead of winter. It was a romantic spot. We were always entertaining and there were no dull moments. In fact, one day as I collected a bundle of sheets and towels for the laundry, I remarked, "Sometimes I feel like I'm back at the Mayfair Motel."

It wasn't meant to be a nasty remark, at all. I loved the Mayfair days and never minded doing any of the work but it provoked a sharp retort from Barb, Ted's daughter. Although I got along well with the rest of Ted's family, she always seemed to resent me. I understood it was hard for her but I was never able to bridge the gap between us. Eileen and I, on the other hand, were good friends. I always thought of her as my adopted daughter and was broken hearted when she died of cancer last year.

One of my favourite cottage stories came about as we were planning what came to be an annual celebration, looked forward to eagerly by friends and family alike.

"Let's have a bang up time on July fourth, this year," Ted said one morning over breakfast. This was our favourite time of day, lingering over coffee and toast after breakfast.

"What do you mean by 'bang up'," I asked, suspiciously. You could not buy fireworks in Maine at that time.

"Just that," replied Ted. Let's do it up big for all the grandchildren. We can drive up to Canada and buy fireworks for the lake."

He was as excited as one of the children when we woke up to a glorious sunny fourth of July that year. Everything was ready for the big barbecue. Hamburgers, hot dogs, buns, salads; potato, tossed and jellied, fried chicken, chocolate cake, apple, rhubarb and blueberry pies—my speciality—and plenty of lemonade and watermelon.

We spent the day swimming, canoeing and playing baseball, eating and visiting with all the extended family and friends who were invited for the celebration. Every bed in the cottage was taken and every bunk we had in the boathouse as well. Finally, the sun went down and we all waited eagerly for the fireworks Ted had promised.

Of course everyone loved the spectacle that year. Both the kids and the grownups were delighted with the roman candles, rockets, multicoloured star bursts and, everyone's favourite, the burning school house, all reflected in the still waters of the lake. "This'll be a hard act to follow," I said to Ted, as we sat around the campfire toasting marshmallows and drinking steaming mugs of hot chocolate.

Chapter 11

South America, Here We Come

Start of our South American trip.

Before Christmas, we made plans for a trip to South America. This time we would be travelling with twelve others on a freighter. Instead of the cramped quarters I expected, we had a spacious suite, a living room, bedroom and bathroom. We soon became accustomed to sea life, which included playing bridge every day with another couple on board. Travelling by freighter was Ted's idea. He read an ad in the paper one morning advertising the 'freighter cruise'. It certainly is a change from life aboard a cruise ship. For one thing, instead of hurrying off the ship in port, we leaned on the guard rails after the ship docked and watched oil being loaded in Georgetown, Guyana. In Macapa, at the mouth of the Amazon, we welcomed a family of missionaries, including their little fair-haired girls with head lice, which their mother said was the result of all the dampness in the air. Head lice! It reminded me of bed bugs, the ones we found in our beds when our family moved from Invermere to New Westminster.

At Belem, we saw houses on stilts and people with horrible lumps all over their bodies. No one could tell us what caused these tumours. As in Bogota, we were not sheltered from real life on this journey.

Rio was a different story. Carnival was in full swing and we had tickets to the biggest ball of the season. We took a taxi to a huge arena with a big ramp out into the middle of the crowd. There were TV cameras everywhere. I saw myself, in a pretty blue ball gown draped from the shoulder, on at least twenty cameras. When they announced the North American guests, ZsaZsa Gabor was only one of the many Hollywood stars among them.

Our taxi driver, who was supposed to come to take us back to the ship, never did find us in the huge crowd. In the end, we walked back, me barefoot, carrying my heels. It might look like fun. It wasn't. Gallant Ted offered to carry me but I walked.

In Sao Paulo we toured the countryside, visiting a snake farm where they milked the snakes for their venom used in making an antidote for snake bites. The snakes were in a virtual snake pit, deep with curved walls to contain the reptiles. I had seen rattlesnakes around Kamloops and was not any more squeamish than most folks, but I had snake nightmares for several nights after that.

Next stop, Montevideo and by hydrofoil across the 'river of silver', the Rio de la Plata, to the beautiful city of Buenos Aires where we saw graffiti covered statues of Juan Peron. An old friend of Ted's, an executive of the National Bank, expecting to meet us, examined all the cruise ship lists for days. He didn't expect us to arrive by freighter. We spoke to him on the phone and he said he'd meet us on the steps of the capital building. He told Ted he had put on quite a bit of weight since they had last seen each other. When we arrived there, I put out my hand out to the biggest man I had ever seen. He was surprised that I knew who he was and, of course, I didn't tell him it was because of his size! He must have weighed at least 250 pounds. He introduced us to a couple at the American Club, who invited us to a meal at their beautiful estancia on a lake out in the cattle country.

Soon we were on our way, crossing the Andes, first by boat and then by train. After we boarded the small boat for the first leg of our journey, a man came to collect our tickets. We didn't have any! The couple right behind us said, "We have a packet of tickets we collected before we left the hotel. Our travel agent told us to do this."

Ted hurried back to the hotel while I watched the crew fire up the wood-burning engine. It was belching huge black cinders. I was wearing a white skirt and Ted, white pants. I pushed a soiled looking jacket to make room for Ted beside me when he returned with our tickets. The owner of the jacket came along just then and snatched up his, by then, filthy jacket.

Before long we were talking to a young couple behind us from South Africa, who spoke Spanish. We shared meals along the way, including barbecued steak, bread and wine, several times at picnic areas. After passing Mount Osorno, we boarded a train to Chile. The station was a funny little building with one lone light bulb hanging from the ceiling.

We shared a flight down to Puerto Montt with the couple from South Africa. Our in-flight meal consisted of stale, hard buns. They passed us a bottle of wine, saying it would help to wash the buns down.

Crossing the Andes.

Scenes on trip to South America.

Scenes and people met in South America.

Margaret and llama in Peru.

Market Place at Cusco.

We were becoming fast friends with Edward and Gillian by then and that night we enjoyed a bottle a wine in their hotel room. Edward, who had a tape recorder, was intrigued with our accents. We found their accents intriguing, too. To our ears, Gillian sounded more Irish than South African.

Edward explained that he was originally from Argentina but had lived in Ireland, where he met Gillian. She had been an actress in the Dublin theatre. I was enchanted with her perfect diction and her lovely Irish lilt. She had beautiful red hair, just a few freckles and gorgeous green eyes.

Ted with Edward and Gillian at San Carlos de Bariloche.

Mount Osorno, South America.

On a night of dancing, she admired my glass shoes and tried them on. They were a little too big for her so when we returned home I found a pair and sent them to her.

After touring the Chilean ruins, we all flew on to Santiago and Valparaiso, then Puerto Montt, where we said good bye to our new friends. They were thinking of leaving South Africa, saying they didn't feel it was going to be a good place to bring up their four boys. Before we parted, they asked us to visit them in South Africa. "Be sure to come by next year," they invited, "Before we leave the country." We had no idea what an invitation it was.

Bolivia and Peru were the next stops. In Lima, we stayed at the hotel where Uncle Ben had stayed when he was working for Standard Oil. He had told us about the poverty in Peru, where restaurant owners saved all the scraps to give to the poor people every day. We could see it was still a country of the very rich and the very poor. This contrast was becoming a familiar sight and it made us uneasy.

Machu Picchu was our next destination. We had looked forward to visiting this Inca site but I was apprehensive about the bus ride high up into the Andes. We planned to stay overnight at the end of the tortuous ride on the winding, narrow road that followed the Urubamba River. Through the window, we saw alpacas grazing on the hillside. "Don't look down," Ted advised. As far as I was concerned, there was no place else to look!

Selling produce in Machu Picchu.

Terraces on Machu Picchu.

Margaret with Peruvian girls.

There was just one room left in the tiny inn when we reached the top. There was very little food available, but we were thankful to have a place to sleep at the end of a very long day.

The next day, a guide took us over the ruins. We walked away up a trail and looked down over the ruins. We passed Indians coming down, carrying large machetes. Some of them pointed at Ted's watch. I was terrified, but all they wanted to know was the time.

On to Cuzco, where we toured the city and the surrounding countryside. At every stop people sold produce, beans, potatoes, fruit, chicken and pigs. The women, dressed in voluminous petticoats and Panama bowler hats, strutted down the streets, often spinning hanks of wool as they chatted amongst themselves. You could buy woven goods in the markets. I began collecting little dolls on this trip and now I have dolls in traditional costumes from all over the world. Whenever children visit, they stand fascinated in front of the glass fronted cabinets and want to know where each doll is from. I always say, "Which one would you like to hold?" and then I take that one down from its shelf and put it in the child's hand. Children always recognize that this is a special privilege and always handle the dolls with care. How much more natural are these dolls compared to the too perfect Barbies you see everywhere here.

Back in Lima, we moved from our hotel to a very posh country club. Although our trip was prepaid in Boston, after we left our ship we were charged for hotels everywhere we went. As soon as I wrote to our travel agent back in Boston, complaining about this, we no longer paid extra for our hotel rooms and I received a dozen red roses at the country club.

An Ecuadoran family.

And, once again, it was distressing to see the very rich against a familiar South American backdrop of very poor people.

We boarded our Grace Line ship, now loaded with perishables, and headed for Ecuador with sixty passengers. We sat with the captain, who was very informative about the Latin American world

Shacks in Colombia.

A Grace Line freighter.

we were leaving behind. While we hung over the railing, fascinated by the huge, seven foot long banana stems being loaded, I thought of Harry Belafonte singing "Dayo, Dayo, Daylight is comin' and me wan' to go home." All the men wore bright bandannas tied around their heads.

Next, we watched coffee being loaded on board in Buenaventura and then took our place in the line-up of ships waiting to sail through the Panama Canal. While we waited, the captain filled the swimming pool with fresh water. He also let me blow the whistle. "Not too short, now," he directed. Because we had fruit on board, we had the right of way and priority over the other ships waiting to pass through the canal. Our last stop was Baranquilla, where the captain accompanied us ashore. This was our opportunity to buy Panama hats and I also bought a funny little doll made of straw.

We were on our way home, at last. When we arrived in New York that morning, after breakfast, when Ted opened our stateroom door, there was a seven foot stem of bananas and two cases of coffee for us to take home. The bananas were as green as grass. Deb and Arthur met us with my car and we had no trouble putting the bananas, along with the coffee, in the trunk of the Caddy.

On our last day at sea, I had a pain in my face which gradually became worse over the following day. Arthur took me to his dentist, who couldn't find anything wrong. I just wanted to go home so Ted drove right to Presque Isle, stopping only for gas. As he was filling up the tank, I went into the bathroom, leaving our camera on the front seat. In the short time it took before we were back in the car, our camera disappeared. We lost a full roll of film of pictures from our trip. It seemed such a shame. In our four months away, no one ever stole anything from us. Now, here we were back in our home state only to have a thief take our camera.

The pain in my face got steadily worse until finally, Ted called our family doctor. He took one look at me and said, "You've got a bad case of jaundice and neuralgia." I had been well all the time we were travelling, never experiencing the dreaded Montezuma's revenge or anything else in South America. Coming home sick and losing our camera and film were disappointing but with a good rest and the warm weather, I was soon well again, with so many happy memories of our trip.

Chapter 12

South Africa

Start of our South African trip.

When I finally sold the Mayfair and left B.C., the only regrets I had were about leaving dear friends behind. I told everyone they must come and visit us in Maine and they did! Connie and Jim McGowan came the next October and stayed with us at Portage Lake. The year before, Ted gave me a 410 shot gun and taught me to use it. That Christmas I gave him a 129 Browning. We took our friends hunting for partridge and we brought down enough of them to have quite a feast in front of the fire that night in the cabin.

We had been exchanging letters with our new South African friends, Gillian and Edward. They repeated their invitation to visit them, saying, once again, to come before they left the country. I had some money from the sale of the motor court and Ted said, "Why not? Who knows when we'll get another opportunity like this one, to have as our guides two people who really know the country."

Ted always said "You never know what tomorrow will bring." He never talked much about his first marriage, but I knew it must have been very difficult for him all those years. He did say, often, that when he met me he knew he'd been given a second chance to find happiness and he felt we should travel as much as possible while we were still relatively young and healthy. So, we drove down to Boston to see our friendly travel agent and booked a passage to South Africa for the following January.

Ted reminded me that it was almost time for the

one-cent sale at the drugstore and Thanksgiving and Christmas would come soon after. To add to the excitement and busyness of the next few months, we decided to sell our house at 27 Hillside Drive and build a new one. We planned to stay out at the cottage for a month before we left on our trip. When we returned, our new house would be waiting for us. Ted bought a new car, a red Saab. "You two are just like a couple of kids in a candy store," one of our friends laughed. We were happy and we just couldn't get enough of each other.

"I hope this never ends," I thought.

Thanksgiving and Christmas are busy times in a small town like Presque Isle. There are bazaars and parties and I had a big family dinner on Christmas Day. As I packed our bags I told Ted that the news about the Mau Mau in Kenya was making me a little nervous. He reassured me, saying that, the newspapers and TV always make it sound worse than it is. "I hope so," I thought. I had a premonition that something was going to go wrong this time, but I didn't say anything more about it to Ted.

We spent New Year's in Connecticut with Ted's brother and his wife and then left our car again with Deb, who drove us to our ship. The *Robin Goodfellow* had carried a thousand troops during the Second World War. It was now carrying heavy machinery, twelve passengers, including four Mennonite missionaries in little white caps and their car. Our only stop, during the long voyage across the Atlantic was in Aruba, for fuel. When we reached the Cape rollers, I was feeling queasy for the first time. The water was rough and the waves high. A steamroller broke loose from its cables and one of the missionaries began shouting that his car would be smashed.

"To hell with your car," the captain shouted back. "What about my ship?"

The crew managed to batten everything down again before we saw our first albatross. It had at least a seven foot wing span. I remembered my father reciting lines from *The Ancient Mariner* and thinking that bird might well be a warning to us.

"Don't be silly," Ted said affectionately. "These birds just live here. You don't really believe in bad omens, do you?"

"Of course not," I replied and meant it, sort of.

Edward's former wife, Doreen, was at the dock to meet us in Cape Town. We had a five hundred mile trip north to where Edward and Gillian lived in the Drakensburg Mountains, and it seemed that Doreen was quite happy to act as hostess this way. I guessed their divorce must have been amicable since Edward was still looking after her financially. When she saw we had a mountain of luggage, because we were not returning to the States until May, she said, "I hope we can fit all your things into the boot."

We had a quick tour of the city before she left us at our hotel, saying, "I'll pick you up in the morning and take you down to the Cape of Good Hope." At the hotel, we were told to put any shoes that needed cleaning outside our door at night. They were polished and back in place the next morning. Our clothes, that needed pressing, were done in no time and we enjoyed tea in our room before breakfast, as well.

"I could learn to like this life," Ted smiled.

On our trip down to the Cape the next morning we saw the most beautiful flowers, including many varieties I was seeing for the first time, and many birds as well. Doreen pointed out an old iron boot. "In the old days of the sailing ships," she said, "people would leave messages in it for their loved ones back in England and Europe."

That night, she invited us for dinner, along with some other South African couples. In the morning, we rode the cable car to Table Mountain, where we had a picnic, packed at our hotel. The panorama below was spectacular and the flowers around us brilliant and exotic.

Ted on Cape Town golf course.

When Doreen learned that we were golfers, she arranged a game for us at her club. Nowadays, every golfer has a motorized cart. Back then, we walked, usually accompanied by a caddy. In Cape Town, our caddy was a young black man, who, after the first hole, took off his shoes and hid them in a hedge. After the eighteenth hole, he ran back and retrieved them.

While we had lunch at the club, we met a couple who offered to take us out to the Paarl Valley the next day, to see the vineyards and wineries. The countryside on the drive out there reminded me of Arizona, dry with red rock bluffs. These people had a huge vineyard. There were several other guests at the lunch, which was more like a dinner. They were obviously very wealthy and very hospitable as well, since they really knew nothing about us. The only thing that bothered me was that, while they talked to us in English, they spoke Afrikaans to their other guests.

Later, when we drove onto a wonderful, white sandy beach, we managed to get the car stuck. Several sunbathers helped push us out, saying, "There are some places one should just not go in a car."

Finally, Doreen put us on a bus to Bloomfontein, where Edward and Gillian met us and took us to their ranch. Edward, who spoke the Zulu language, arranged for us to have a meal with the local witch doctor.

What an experience! The witch doctor was very rich and lived with his 22 wives in a hexagon-shaped house.

Zulu Greeting.

Edward and Margaret with witch doctor and eight of his 22 wives.

Margaret and Gillian with witch doctor and wives.

Young boys selling mushrooms.

Young girls.

Edward speaking with young girls in Khosa, their official language.

Left: Mother and son.
Right: Traveling companions.

He greeted us, wearing a leopard skin and invited us to sit at any one of the many tables each set for eight withfine English china in many different patterns. Ted and Gillian sat at one, and Edward and I at another. Servants brought each table a chicken with many vegetables, most of which we had never tasted before. There was so much food, I wondered how we could possibly make even a small dent in it. And, if we didn't eat enough, would our host be offended?

While we ate, the witch doctor's 22 wives entertained us with singing, accompanying themselves on African stringed instruments. Later, Ted explained to the doctor he, too, was in the 'medicine business', pointing out that our host was much better paid with cattle and horses. "What do you do if your people can't pay?" Ted asked.

The doctor showed Ted a long piece of wool, which he said he put around their necks and stretched it until it broke. We could see, just beyond a barbed-wire fence, many men breaking rocks in the hot sun. Did these men, literally slaves, owe a debt they couldn't pay? We never found out.

The next day, Edward flew us in his private plane up to a trading station he owned at the headwaters of the Orange River. A Scottish couple, Mr. and Mrs. Wallace, managed it for him. The natives came there to buy sugar, flour and tea. Mrs. Wallace dried fruit and vegetables in the hot sun. "It's the best way to preserve them," she told us. She was delighted with our visit, saying they were starved for the company of white folk.

Curious natives.

Rondevals and carral.

Father and children.

Plane to the Orange River.

Alternative transportation.

Customers at Edward's trading station.

The Orange River region is a diamond mining area, and, when we returned to Edward's ranch, he took us to Kimberley to see one of the mines. We watched the ore being sluiced through a trough and then through a greasy mixture to which the diamonds stuck. The men who work in the mines are searched at the end of every shift.

Back at the ranch, Edward had another surprise in store for us. After picking up a young black girl, who had rows of coloured beads around her neck and, who was sitting under a tree with a can of snuff, he drove us down to his cottage on the coast to go shark fishing. Gillian said the girl would do the washing and cleaning for us at the beach. I wasn't so sure I wanted this, preferring to wash my delicate lingerie myself. But, no, it would not do, so I gave her my clothes. Later I saw them neatly laid out on the grass in the sun to dry. I was horrified when I saw cattle wandering nearby, but none of them trampled the washing.

Edward and Gillian had other servants as well, and one young woman had a baby, it's shiny black skin covered in white spots. Was it measles?

Gillian packed a picnic lunch for us and we were off shark fishing from Shark's Rock. Because neither Gillian nor I were strong enough to fight a shark at the end of a line, Ted and Edward were the only ones actually fishing. Wearing leather gloves with gauntlets, they threw a bucket of blood into the water, hoping to lure the sharks. The men caught one shark that afternoon, while the women chatted in the warm sun.

Fishing for shark.

Back at the cottage, I wanted nothing as much as a warm shower. Gillian handed me towels and directed me to a silo-shaped structure with a ladder up one side. Once I was in the shower, a boy climbed up the ladder and another boy passed up bucketfuls of water, which he dumped on me. Instead of turning off the tap, you yelled, "Stop!" It's amazing how white the towels were. I guess the hot African sun bleaches and purifies them.

When Gillian and Edward said goodbye to us at Port Elizabeth, I felt uneasy. Since our arrival there had been something strange about Edward with which I was not quite comfortable. Then, the night before we left, Ted confided quietly that Edward had asked him to take twenty-five thousand dollars back to the States for him. When Ted refused, Edward was angry. They had been gone only moments when the police approached us. It was obvious that they had followed us.

The police suspected Edward of smuggling diamonds. They questioned us carefully and suggested we be wary of any dealings with him in the future. We were shocked and felt betrayed. We realized then, that Edward and Gillian's friendliness in South America was probably part of a scam. They, no doubt, had spotted us as looking honest enough to get away with money smuggling. That was the reason they invited us to South Africa and the reason, also, that Doreen had entertained us so generously in Cape Town.

"Whew!" said Ted, after the police left. "Can you imagine where we'd be right this minute if I'd agreed to smuggle the money?"

I shuddered to think. "Nevertheless," I thought, "They did show us an Africa most people never get to see."

Edward must have thought us quite naïve. I can honestly say, though, that of all the people we met on our many travels, Edward and Gillian were the only ones who proved devious.

Glad to put some distance between ourselves and our 'friends', we took the garden route up the coast to Durban, a colourful city with a large East Indian population. In the market, you could buy curries of a dozen different strengths. It was there I purchased my two beautiful saris and rode for the first time in a rickshaw.

Rickshaw in Durban.

Our next stop was Kruger National Park and its promise of African wildlife. We were disappointed to learn that no one could tour the park without a guide and that no guide was available. Finally, the park authorities made an exception, on the condition that we follow closely behind another couple and their guide. We stopped for the mandatory 'elevenses' and lunch, before heading on to the famous Tree Tops Lodge. We arrived just as Mary Pickford was leaving!

Beneath the lodge, built high on stilts, elephants came for the salt lick, followed by funny little warthogs.

Above: Tree Tops, where we stayed. Below: Oxen dragging nontaxable shed.

From Durban, we took a flight to Johannesburg, where we visited with Edward's mother and her sister.

"Do you think we should see them, under the circumstances?" I asked Ted.

"I don't see how we can back out now," Ted replied. I worried. That albatross was still out there somewhere.

That evening, when we sat down to play bridge, I realized that we were playing not just for points but for money. I was afraid we would lose our shirts, but we had good hands. We left as soon as we could do so politely, saying we were slated for an early start the next morning.

"Whew, again!" Ted said, back at out hotel. "We are seeing a totally different side of this country than I had ever dreamed."

"Honestly," I replied. "To think we thought Edward

and Gillian were such nice people." We hadn't seen the last of them.

The next day we visited a gold mine surrounded in barbed wire. We donned overalls, boots and miner's headbands to light our way as we descended in an elevator, over a mile down into a mine shaft called Margaret Shaft. A strong smell of urine greeted us as we walked and walked uphill to see the veins of gold. Every time a car filled with ore passed us, we flattened ourselves against the wall to let it by.

Ready to go down Margaret Shaft, Johannesburg.

We learned that the miners, all blacks, were virtually prisoners, hired on for eighteen months and then dismissed. They lived in shacks, forbidden to leave the site. This meant they could not see their families during that time. They all wanted to earn just enough money to pay for a few cattle and to find wives. We were horrified.

Believe me, I was glad when we were, once again, in the fresh air at the top of the shaft, where we showered and changed into our clothes. My clean white dress felt so good.

The manager of the smelter was a friend of Ted's brother, Bob, and the smelter parts were made in Westport, Connecticut where Bob worked. The metal came out in little gold bars, just pure gold.

Out next stop was Pretoria, the capital of South Africa, with its beautiful pink limestone capital buildings on a high hill looking over the city. The protea, the national flower of South Africa, was everywhere in many colours. The city, with its beautiful buildings and abundant flowers, was such a contrast to 'Cardboard Town', where the blacks lived in squalid shacks, so crowded together it was hard to understand how they could exist at all.

From Pretoria we flew to Victoria Falls. We could hear the sound of the falls from miles away. For the next few nights we slept, cocooned in our beds, under mosquito netting. By day we travelled down the Zambezi River, watching monkeys playing in the trees. At dawn one morning, we flew over the countryside in a small plane, where below us, was a sight I will never forget, herds of elephants, buffaloes, wildebeasts, Thompson gazelles and antelopes.

Then we visited friends in Rhodesia and Kenya. We visited the Nairobi Game Park, where our friends drove us right up to a pride of lions, first issuing a warning, "You must not get out of the car." We didn't! However, I was still able to take some excellent pictures of the lions as well as zebra and rhinos.

Pretoria, capital of South Africa.

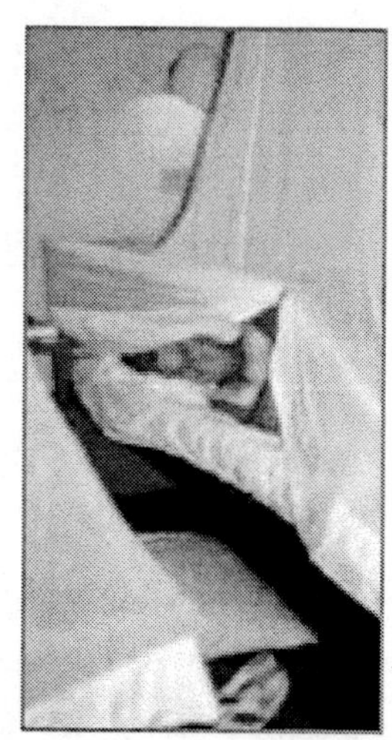

Under mosquito netting.

Traffic on the road.

Victoria Falls.

At Lake Nakuru we saw millions of flamingos standing in lime water, before we went down into the Rift Valley. We were invited to stay at the posh Mount Kenya Safari Club and then flew over rugged terrain to Addis Ababa where we met one of Ted's old school chums, now flying for the Ethiopian airlines.

In 1961, Haile Selassi was still in power. In South Africa, particularly in the mines, we knew the native people were treated inhumanely and in Rhodesia we knew the blacks were considered the servant class. In Ethiopia, we saw evidence of a harsh system of justice. Two men were hanging by their feet in the town square. We left Ethiopia in a plane decorated inside in blue silk emblazoned with the Lion of Judah, but for as long as I live, when I think of Ethiopia, I will see those bodies hanging in that square.

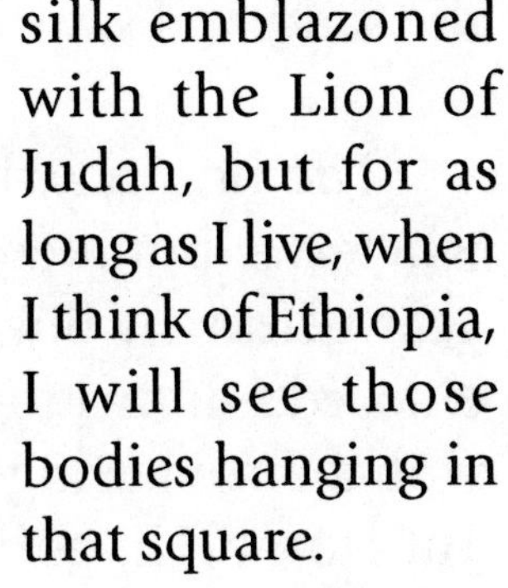

Above: Kenya.
Both below: Nairobi Game Park.

Egypt was our last stop in Africa. After we settled into our large hotel room right beside the Nile in Cairo, Ted was busy trying to track down our big suitcase that we had sent on ahead of us. Finally, with the help of the American Embassy, he located our bag and we were free to see the sights. First stop, of course, was El Giza and the pyramids. Bending over to climb up into the royal chamber of the second largest pyramid, I began to feel claustrophobic. The entrance was narrow. It was so much smaller than I expected and I was glad to get out of there and ride a camel to the Sphinx. We visited Memphis where we rode little donkeys, saw mummies buried in the sand and saw the step pyramids.

The next day, in Cairo, we headed for the market, where we bumped into some people we had met the year before in Buenos Aires. What a small world! We enjoyed a dinner together and spent a day at the museum with them, viewing the many ancient treasures from King Tut's tomb. His golden mask revealed the face of a young boy. His furniture, chairs, and tables, and his jewellery, the things that surrounded him in his every day life, brought him a little closer.

As we climbed wearily into bed that night, Ted said sleepily, "Those people we met seemed nice but I'm just as glad they didn't invite us to visit them."

"I know just what you mean," I chuckled.

The next day we flew 400 miles up the Nile to Luxor to see King Tut's tomb in the Valley of the Kings. That night it was very cold. We had seen men out on the desert huddled around braziers to keep warm. At our hotel, again on the banks of the Nile, our guard slept on the floor outside our door, protecting us from who knows what! I sensed some kind of danger and was glad not to be left alone.

Left top: Pyramids of Giza.

Above: Traveling to the Sphinx.

Left: Entrance to King Tut's tomb in the Valley of the Kings.

Queen Hatshepsut's tomb.

In the morning, we saw the vivid reds and blues of the paintings in King Tut's tomb and the beautiful temple of the Goddess, Hatshepsut. The huge, carved columns of the temple of Karnak really made us feel insignificant in time and place. Seeing a donkey turning a water wheel to pump water and farmers throwing grain in the air to separate wheat from chaff as we sailed back up the Nile made us realize that nothing ever changes in those ancient places. At that moment, we saw another temple being moved to make way for the Aswan Dam.

Recently, I read about a terrible fire aboard just such a train as the crowded one we took back to Cairo at four the next morning. We were the only white folk among many men with prayer beads. The head of the dining car took us to a private dining car. All the china was turned upside down. It was the only way to keep the desert sand from settling on it. Our waiter wore a clean, white apron; the others wore filthy ones. We had boiled eggs, fresh from the nest just as the hens had laid them. "Don't worry, "Ted told me." The eggs are clean enough on the inside."

By the time we got back to our hotel, I had a very sore throat. Ted had some soup sent up, waiter and all. He was dressed as if from the Arabian nights, with shoes that turned up at the toes with little bells on them. He stayed to make sure I drank all of my soup!

While I rested, Ted found out that our ship, *The American Export*, was going to be a day late so we spent a day in Alexandria before boarding and heading home. The ship was a freighter with ninety passengers.

Oxen and water wheel.

Chapter 13
At the Captain's Table

Being asked to sit at the captain's table is something I'd never seen myself doing before I started travelling with Ted. By this time, though, we had enjoyed several dinners with a variety of captains. Some of them invited us up on the bridge to see life behind the wheel, behind the scenes both on cruise ships as well as passenger-carrying freighters. I think it helped that we were good conversationalists and obviously a happy couple. These are qualities that appeal to captains, who must appear as good hosts but not as available for short term liaisons with single female passengers. Most of the captains we had the good fortune to meet were ordinary family men who knew that a certain amount of bonhomie was a necessary part of their role aboard. And, they knew they had to look the part as well. Back then, it was a real coup to have your picture taken with the captain in full uniform. Imagine our surprise then, when, after our ship left Alexandria and we had been at sea for a few hours, we were joined in the lounge by a rather shabby gentleman wearing baggy pants and a shabby gray sweater with a huge hole in the elbow. When I asked him what he did, he informed us he was the ship's captain. He certainly did not look the part, but, once again, we were invited to his table in the dining lounge.

He was affable, though. When we told him we wanted to buy a rug for our new house, he offered to accompany us to a rug market in our next stop, Beirut.

"One thing, you must remember," he advised us. "You must accept the merchant's hospitality. He will offer you coffee and you will offend him if you refuse."

In the bazaar, there were so many rugs to choose from, all colours and sizes. The one we finally chose, while drinking tiny cups of very strong Turkish coffee, was a beautiful blue Royal Kerman, an odd size, 13 by 17. Because one end was not quite finished, the dealer showed me how to tie the knots at one end. Our rumpled captain arranged for the rug to be sent to the ship, where a crew member rolled it out on the companion way and then rolled it up again around a long pole. Finally two burly crewmen stashed it in the hold. We would not see it again until we arrived in New York. Of course, Ted and I understood that our friendly captain was probably getting a share in what we paid for the rug. This was, after all, the Middle East. And, whatever the deal, it was nothing compared to the one proposed to us by Edward.

When I read about all the trouble in the Middle East, I think back with sadness, to the beautiful city that was Beirut back in the 1960s. Lebanon was known as the land of milk and honey. The weather there, on the shores of the Mediterranean, was balmy. Olive trees were everywhere you looked. The campus of the American University was truly beautiful. The city seemed so elegant and civilized, the people gracious.

One day, we went to Baalbek, an ancient Phoenician city that at one time was colonized by the Greeks and Romans. The Greeks called it Heliopolis, or city of the sun and it was there that we saw cannon balls imbedded in the old walls, proof that strife of one kind or another has been a frequent visitor in that part of the world.

The next stamp on our passport was Greek, our next stop Piraeus and Athens. Travelling by freighter has its own serendipity. Sometimes you are in a port for less than a day, and at other times, you may have several days to explore a city. We had a few days layover in Athens and decided, rather than staying on shipboard, we would join another couple at the Saint George Hotel. Visiting the birthplace of western philosophy, science, and culture was an education for me and Ted, an amateur archaeologist, was an excellent guide and teacher.

Ted knew, soon after we met, about my abbreviated education. I mentioned earlier that I was very worried about meeting his family, who had all attended university. Whenever I voiced my apprehension about mixing with educated people, Ted would always say, "Honestly, hon, you don't have a thing to be ashamed about. For one thing, to our ears, that Canadian accent of yours makes you sound like a duchess. And you carry yourself like a princess."

I guess I have my parents to thank for that. Both were sticklers for clear diction and good grammar. Like most parents of their day, they never missed an opportunity to correct anything that to their ears smacked of sloppy language. They brought from England a steamer trunk full of good grammar, clear diction, excellent posture and good manners. Not to mention honesty, fair play and a good work ethic.

"How many times have I told you, it's 'going', not goin'," I can still hear my mother say. "And while we're at it, stand up straight, missy!"

"Keep your voices down! Everything in moderation!"

Good grooming was as important as good grammar. Betty and I brushed our hair a hundred strokes every night at bedtime, pushed back the cuticles on our carefully filed fingernails and even walked around with books balanced on our heads as we learned to walk like ladies.

I know, too, that, had they lived, they would have educated us to the best of their ability. For Betty and I, they gave us all we needed for living successfully. Poor Jack, though. He just resented the corrections, lectures and direct orders to "Take your elbows off the table! Why can't you stand up straight, for heavens sake!" and "I must have told you at least a hundred times, to look at me when I'm speaking to you." With every word, Jack's face became more and more resentful.

Betty and I didn't like being corrected this way, either, but somehow, we understood that our parents were teaching us good manners and good graces. And they did! To this day, both of us can go anywhere and mix with anyone. With Ted as my guide, I eventually lost my self-consciousness about my lack of formal education.

Although Ted was a highly successful pharmacist, his real love was archaeology. His father had been a pharmacist and expected Ted to carry on the family business, so archaeology became Ted's passion away from work. And, if archaeology could be worked into a business trip, so much the better. I suppose, when I look back on all our travels, the ones that gave us the most pleasure were the ones to these ancient sites. Ted always read and researched extensively before we left home and his passion for the subject made him an entertaining and instructive companion. In fact, once he got started, there was no stopping him. It was one of the many things I loved about him.

First lecture in the hot and crowded city of Athens was the Parthenon. "Just think of it," Ted said to me.

"Here we are standing on the very site of a temple erected in 400 B.C. E., to honour the goddess Athena! And the outer structure is still standing!"

I may not have had much formal education, but I was certainly making up for that now. I was a quick learner and paid close attention, as Ted pointed out the Doric columns and the Temple of Zeus.

"This is the birthplace of western philosophy," he told me. "This is where all our science, culture and art were born," he added as we stood looking down at the Acropolis.

Ted insisted that we take time to have fun after the serious business of sightseeing. While we were in Athens, we joined our friends every evening in a little taverna near our hotel. The food was delicious and our host played the balalaika as we ate succulent pieces of lamb and delicious lemon roasted potatoes. Feta cheese, olives and green peppers, humous and Greek wine complemented the main course. However, I never really learned to drink ouzo or retsina.

After Greece, it seemed fitting that our next stop would the Rome of Bernini and Michelangelo.

St. Peter's was built to overawe and, in its sheer size, it does. How strange to enter this huge church and inside find so intimate a sculpture as Michelangelo's Pieta. From the overwhelming experience of St. Peter's Square, I moved inside to find myself standing in front of an incredibly sad moment in time, just a mother holding her beloved son. In some ways, Rome does not seem such a holy city.

Everyone hurries, and even St. Peter's often bustles

with the rush of churchmen attending a mass, and tourists, guidebooks in hand, moving from one 'must see' to another.

Outside the Vatican, cars and motorbikes whiz by. Romans walk quickly and purposefully amid still more tourists, eager to make every moment of their stay in the Holy City count. The water flowing and splashing from the many fountains encourages one to slow down amid all this bustle, but the place I found most calming were the Borghese Gardens. That's where I saw the cats everywhere. Sitting in the sun, curled up in the hedges, peeking out from behind columns, there must be more stray cats in Rome than anywhere else I've ever visited. Later we saw more in the Colosseum and even more in the English Cemetery, where many well-known English writers were buried during the 1800's.

We took a train to Florence and I will never forget standing on Piazzale Michelangelo, looking down over the red tiled roofs of the city, and the magnificent dome of the Duomo, spotting Santa Croce, the trees in bloom throughout the city and the Uffizi gallery, where Lorenzo di Medici once governed this beautiful city. Everyone in Florence seemed so happy and easygoing. It was hard to imagine the Bonfire of the Vanities, which Ted described to me.

"Imagine, Margaret!" he said, "They burned all their books and many personal treasures and priceless works of art, so compelling was a fanatical priest named

Savonarola." It was hard to believe. Even harder to believe was the terrible damage caused when the Arno flooded Florence in 1966, just a few short years after we visited the city.

After brief stops Marseilles and Barcelona, we were crossing the Atlantic and on our way home again. What a trip it had been! I had learned so much. But the best thing about this trip, which took us through Africa from Cape Town to Alexandria, and through the Mediterranean from Beirut to Barcelona, was just being with Ted. He was such an easy man to love. I wished that our lives could go on together, forever.

Chapter 14

A New House

Back at home we couldn't wait to get back to the cottage. I guess I always loved pushing rocks around and there was plenty of that to do in making a garden on our property there. It sloped down to the lake and there was a lovely little creek with delicate ferns growing along its banks. Ted and I decided to build a lily pond and when it was finished, we planted lady slippers that we found in the woods nearby. After we levelled the back of the property we built a rock wall, just like the ones we had seen in the Lake District on our trip to England, and we also built a rockery. We decided to move up to the lake while our house in Presque Isle was being built, so we put all our furniture in storage and settled down to enjoy a cottage summer.

Everything about the move and the house building was moving along so smoothly and we were enjoying the cottage life when our beloved doggies were both killed by a truck backing out of our driveway. The boys in the truck were horrified when they saw the dogs lying on the driveway. I was heartbroken; the dogs had become such pals. Even with all the hubub of moving and construction projects, I found myself grieving for them.

And then, darling Ted came home one night with a little black and white ball of fluff, full of beans, a poodle we named André. "I don't like you being alone out here," Ted explained.

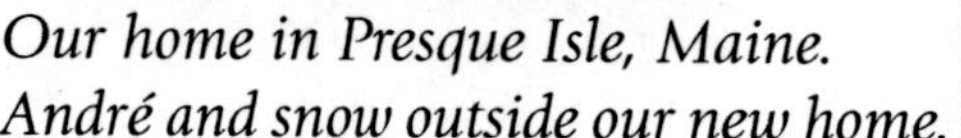

Our home in Presque Isle, Maine.
André and snow outside our new home.

I took André with me everywhere. After the dogs were run over, I just didn't dare to let the little fellow out of my sight, I was so afraid something would happen to him, too. He was my constant companion from then on.

André proved to be an intelligent companion in the bush as well. He always knew when partridges were nearby but if he spotted one he would never bark. He just sat perfectly still, listening.

Losing the dogs was just the first thing to go wrong in 1961. A few months later dear Uncle Ben died, on Betty's birthday, while staying with his brother, Tracy, in Alberta. Back in 1947, I had visited Tracy on his ranch, where he let me ride one of his gentle horses. I pictured Uncle Ben, there, glad that he had been with Tracy at the end. I felt so sad, knowing he had never really healed the rift with his children after his divorce. They were the poorer for that. Ben had been like a father to both Betty and me. We loved him and cherished the memories of all the good times we had together. I know he was happy about my marriage to Ted, remembering the many times he said, "Your way too young, Margaret, to be single the rest of your life. You need to find someone to love and who will love you, in return."

I knew I would never forget Uncle Ben. He was a very dear man.

That fall, while we were building our new house, I started back to school again. Not to pick up where my education left off but to show my slides of Africa to the children in the local school. Presque Isle was a small town and there weren't many globetrotters amongst the folk there. I was an enthusiastic photographer and I enjoyed telling the children about our trip to Africa. Of course, I left out the part about Gillian and Edward wanting us to smuggle the money out of the country!

I always included lots of time for questions and some of them were humdingers! When I showed them the slide of Treetops in Kenya, some little kid was sure to ask "Where is the bathroom." I once heard an astronaut talk about answering children's questions and the one about the bathroom always came up for him, too.

Recently I sat down with some friends to choose some of my slides for this book. I remember the ones of our trip to Africa that the school children always asked about. Although since the time we took our trip, travel to Africa has become quite common, it was still unusual back in the sixties. There were not so many shows about African wildlife on TV, but most of us had seen pictures of the African people and animals in the National Geographic. I remember poring over those pictures when the postman brought us each new issue. I could never imagine being lucky enough to see the tribal women with the neck rings or the women with their lips stretched so strangely.

The children loved to see the pictures of the African people and to hear about the elephants coming to the water hole. They always wanted to know about the giraffes. Did they ever lie down? Had I ever seen a real live gorilla? And, of course the inevitable questions about hunting. Would someone really kill that beautiful lioness with her little cubs?

About hunting, I admit I'm ambivalent. I would never have shot any animal on our safari with anything more dangerous than a camera. However, Ted and I both had rifles at the cottage and regularly went out partridge hunting. What was the difference? Most of the children to whom I was speaking had fathers who hunted. Partridge and duck as well as freshly caught fish, were staples at most dinner tables in Presque Isle. One fall, around that time, I shot a deer. I was sorry, immediately and really began to think about why I could kill a partridge, which would make a good meal, and yet felt so sorry that I had killed a deer.

That fall in Maine was beautiful and the lake was like a mirror, reflecting all the colours of the trees. There were always ducks on the lake and as dusk settled on the quiet waters, we could hear the loons calling. There was an early snowfall that year. I remember feeling so sleepily happy as Ted and I drove home to the cottage from the last country club dance of the season. I was busy, now, making curtains and bedspreads for the new house, and with the sewing and school visits, the time just flew by. I was working quickly as the December 18th moving day was fast approaching. I guess I was just in too much of a hurry, because, one afternoon I caught my finger in the machine. The needle went right through my nail and the pain was excruciating.

Early in December, Ted had a big sign made that said "Merry Christmas Ted and Margaret From Santa Claus." I felt it was a Christmas greeting to all those people in Presque Isle who had made one feel so much a part of the community. We knew they all wanted a tour of our new house and because we had a lot to do to settle in, we decided not to go south in the New Year.

It was such a feeling of satisfaction to see the house take shape. I have a very good sense of spaces and the house turned out just the way I had planned. There was a big stone fireplace, opening into both the living and the family rooms. Four steps down from the living room, the family room opened out to a swimming pool and a garden. The kitchen and breakfast rooms were at the front of the house, so we could look out and see the rest of the world go by. The beautiful rug we bought in Beirut was the focal point of the living room and my newly made bedspreads and matching curtains in the bedrooms were just as I had imagined.

We spent the spring settling in and in May were off to Vancouver, by way of Montreal, for my niece, Carol's wedding. Carol was a truly beautiful bride and a lovely young woman. Betty, her mom, looked so proud of her as we saw the young couple off to Hawaii for their honeymoon. Betty, Art and Ted and I drove down to Seattle to the World's Fair, stayed to see the sights and go up in the famous space needle for dinner, and then Ted and I left for home.

There was another surprise from Edward and Gillian, when we opened our mail back home. They were sending us a young visitor from Ireland, Gillian's home. They had not asked us about this and without giving us any warning, expected us to meet him in New York. There wasn't time to get there by the time we received their letter, so Ted phoned his sister and asked her to meet the young man.

"I guess the kid can't help it, that Edward's a crook," Ted said.

His sister put him on a bus and Sean arrived one very hot day in June.

I took pity on him the minute he stepped off the bus in his very hot Harris tweed jacket and wool pants. We liked him right away, in spite of being angry at Edward and Gillian for putting us in the position of entertaining him with no notice. As we drove up to the cottage, Sean told us he was a fourth year engineering student at the University of Dublin. To our ears, he didn't sound like an Irishman at all. He told us his father was English and his mother Irish, and that they spent most of their time in England, until his father had retired in Ireland.

Ted knew the right people to ask when our young visitor said he would like to work while in the US. He was soon working for Maine Public Service at their generating plant.

It was a very busy summer at the lake, with Sean and most of Ted's family at the cottage. As we got to know Sean better, the saga of Edward and Gillian unfolded. It seems they were neighbours of Sean's parents in Ireland. One day Edward took Sean on a wild ride to Cork to pick up Edward's car, which was arriving from Africa. Sean followed Edward back home, wondering if he should even be trying to keep up with this maniac at the wheel of the other car. When they arrived back in Kilkenny and when Edward had the car safely inside the garage, he tore the seat covers away from the back seat of his Rover, revealing all kinds of South African money hidden behind them.

Chapter 15

A Year in the Life

At the end of August every year we drove over to the Maritimes for a week to where, as Ted was a member of the Maritime Seniors Golf Association, we golfed at the Aroostook Valley Country Club. The golf course there is in the state of Maine, while the clubhouse is in Canada. This unusual arrangement dates back to the days of prohibition in the States, so the members of the club could have a drink after a game.

The Seniors Golf Association also held tournaments in all the Atlantic Provinces, in Charlottetown, Digby Pines, Nova Scotia, and St. Andrews, New Brunswick. The day would end with a lobster dinner, the men all in formal, scarlet jackets and the women in long gowns. After dinner, there was always a dance.

Martime Seniors' Golf Club party.

I was getting to be quite a good golfer myself, by this time, even winning the club championship in 1962 and, of course, Ted and I loved to dance.

That year, we left Sean behind in Presque Isle. He had a surprise waiting for us when we returned. We drove into our garage and saw our second car, a Saab, minus all its doors. Sean had all the parts out on the garage floor. What on earth made him do it? We'll never know, but fortunately he was able to put them all back on again with no parts left over.

Sean told us he would never forget the summer he spent with us. He was especially proud that when we flew into Fish Lake, he caught more fish than anyone. Finally, though, it was time for him to leave. We decided to show him a little of Quebec and Montreal before driving him back down through New England to New York. It was fun retracing the route we took on that last trip, when we were first married and fun showing him the outdoor ovens in which the Québéçois baked their bread, the shrine at Ste. Anne de Beaupré, where many people claimed they had been healed, and taking him up the Saguenay River. After we left him at his hotel in New York, Ted and I drove back home, looking forward to some time on our own again. Much as we enjoyed playing hosts to the many visitors to the cabin, we were always glad to be alone together. That never changed.

On my birthday that year, there was a ball at the country club. Before the dance, we invited sixty of our friends to a cocktail party at our new house.

Every holiday during the year, we gathered the family around us for a celebration. I knew this would be one of my greatest joys when I married Ted.

I'll admit that my schooling was cut short and that I was probably not a first class student. I left that to Betty, my brilliant older sister. I do think, though, the United States does a better job of making their history come to life for children and adults. I always thought history was boring until I moved to Maine. There, even the youngest child knows about the Pilgrim Fathers and the first Thanksgiving.

I hadn't paid much attention to Thanksgiving before I married Ted. For one thing, in Canada the holiday didn't have the same significance, and also, our Canadian Thanksgiving was in October, whereas in the U.S., it is at the end of November. When I was growing up in New Westminster, I suppose Thanksgiving was more of a religious event. Certainly we went to church on the Sunday but the feast day in the church calendar was Harvest Thanksgiving. In the U.S., on the other hand, it is really a day when people remember the first settlers who, helped by the Indians with gifts of corn and turkey, had thankfully survived their first year in the new world.

When I was a child we didn't have much money for Christmas and, since mother and father were both English, our family traditions were not the same as those of my classmates. Yet, we had fun decorating the house with holly from the garden and buying and wrapping little gifts for each other. The services at our church were central to our celebrations. First we always attended the Nine Lessons and Carols to hear the familiar story of the birth of Jesus, to listen to the choir and to join lustily in the carols. Then, on Christmas Eve we always attended the midnight service and had hot chocolate and cookies at home afterwards. Christmas morning we opened our presents and had a delicious dinner of turkey and trimmings.

After our parents passed away, Betty and I dreaded Christmas. One year we received a food hamper from our church. You would think that it would have helped us but, although we were grateful for the food, it just made us feel more wretched than ever. We tried always to pretend that we were managing very well on our own.

When Jack and I married, I was determined to make Christmas a joyful time. Jack tried his best to spoil things. When Uncle Ben joined us, even Jack knew better than to ruin Christmas Day. I always cooked a traditional dinner including plum pudding that I always made myself. Trifle was another typically English tradition. We had a Christmas tree with the prettiest decorations I could find.

Our first Christmas in our new house was everything I had imagined. It was such fun buying gifts for the family, decorating the house, and planning dinner for twenty-two! I was getting to know Ted's family, which was growing all the time. I hoped I could remember everyone's name. I loved entertaining, still do, for that matter and each year, after our first Christmas, I would be busy for weeks ahead, decorating the house, baking and making lists for Christmas gifts for everyone.

I looked at Ted, at the other end of the table with the whole family seated around him as he carved the turkey. In the glow of the candlelight, I said my own little thank you prayer, because I felt so lucky.

When things became too hectic, I'd sit in a favourite chair and do my needlework for a bit. It's something I do, even today, and it never fails to centre me in a calm place, no matter what else is going on around me. I take a project with me wherever I go and it's a conversational opener with strangers.

"Aren't you worried about straining your eyes?" is often the first question they ask.

My answer is, "Not at all. In fact my eye doctor tells me it's what is responsible for my excellent eyesight at 84!"

I suppose it's a case of 'use it or lose it'. Far from weakening the eyes, doing needlework strengthens the eyes. I'm living proof of that. I still do all my own cooking, work in the garden, drive a car and manage my own affairs. I know I'm lucky to have such good health but I know doing so much for myself has kept me young and in good shape. I swim and lawn bowl, too! I guess you could say I'm living my life!

It was Mrs. Archibald who taught me needlework and she was an excellent teacher. When it comes to counted cross-stitch and needlepoint, there is definitely a right way and a wrong way to do it. Don't ask me to tell you about some of the mistakes I've made. Every needle worker has a horror story to tell.

Every Christmas in Presque Isle was a happy one. I counted my blessings, over and over again, that after all those lean years after our parents died, and after my struggles with Jack, here I was, right in the midst of a ready made family, absolutely content with my life.

Chapter 16

Carol

I don't know why we didn't go up to the lake after Boxing Day that year, for a few quiet days on our own. Perhaps it was our pleasure in the new house that made us stay put. I was still in my housecoat, sitting in front of fire, working on my latest needlework project, when the phone rang. It was Betty. Carol was dead.

Betty was sobbing so much that I could hardly make sense of what she was saying. The day suddenly went dark, while I tried to understand what my sister was saying. Carol had only been married a few months. She and her new husband were living in Arizona.

Carol suffered from asthma for many years. I know that now, even when there are many new medications for asthma, it kills people. I read recently of a young man who died in Toronto. He was suffering from an acute attack of asthma and was turned away from two hospitals with overcrowded emergency departments. When I read this in the paper, Carol's tragic death came back to me in seconds. Then, about the only treatment was living in a dry climate and using an inhaler, which helped clear the mucus from the lungs. To this day, we still don't know what happened to Carol. Perhaps the many asthma attacks she suffered for years weakened her heart. She was the dearest girl, pretty and vivacious, kind and thoughtful as well as talented.

I was numb. The day literally went dark. One of the worst Atlantic storms ever was gearing up for a typical mid-winter blast of the East Coast. Ted got on the phone right away to get a flight to Vancouver for me. The only one available was from Montreal. Then, because he knew I was in a state of shock, he called my friend, Phoebe, to help me pack. I can't remember much of the trip to Montreal except that the weather was beginning to close in as Ted drove north. We didn't talk much and when we arrived at Dorval, there was hardly any time before my flight for us to say anything but good-bye. I don't remember anything of the trip across the country except having to change planes not once, but three times, in Toronto, Winnipeg and Calgary.

Art met me at the airport in Vancouver. As he drove me home he told me that Betty and Carol's husband, Jerry were due to arrive from Arizona, later in the day. In fact, we were barely in the door when the phone rang. It was Betty, calling form the airport. Art made another airport run, leaving me to get settled and start to get a meal ready for the four of us. It was a good thing. Keeping busy was the only way I'd be of any use to them at this terrible time.

Ted called from a house south of Montreal to say he

was stranded. Whiteouts up and down the coast were making the highways impassable.

"I might as well have gone with you, hon," he said. "I'm not much use to anyone here." The reason he hadn't flown out with me was that he liked to give his pharmacy staff time off around Christmas. Things were quiet at the store, at that time, except for the usual influenza and bronchitis cases, so he ran the store alone. The staff appreciated this and were always willing to put in extra hours if necessary, at other times of the year. He was right, I needed him with me, but I knew he had done the right thing in trying to get back to Presque Isle.

I got busy and made some sandwiches after I talked to Ted. Then I went into Carol's bedroom and looked at all the photographs on her dresser. There she was, a smiling little girl in a bathing suit, at Paul Lake. Another showed her in her graduation gown, proudly holding her diploma, and in a pretty dress at a high school prom. Finally, there she was a beautiful bride, in June, just a few months ago. "How could she be gone," I asked myself. "What kind of a universe was this, anyway, if such a talented, sweet young woman could be dead?"

The funeral service was huge. Carol had made so many friends growing up in Deep Cove and Betty and Art had many friends as well. Art loved Carol as much as if she were his own daughter, and, in fact, he saw her grow from a cute little youngster into a wonderful young woman. Jerry, Carol's husband, was devastated. He was still in a state of shock but Betty was better off, in some ways. She couldn't stop crying, but at least she was able to mourn Carol's death. I could see that Jerry, who bottled everything inside, would be a long time coming to grips with the tragedy.

After the funeral, Ted and I drove with Betty and Art down to Phoenix to where Carol and Jerry had been living. Betty would have to pack up all Carol's things once the long, tearful drive down there was over. It was one of the hardest things we ever had to do.

Once we sent Carol's things back home, we persuaded Betty and Art to join us in Palm Desert. Betty had her paints with her and started almost right away to paint a picture for us, of the beautiful smoke trees. Betty gave us the picture and it hangs in my house to this day. Both Betty and I find a release in painting and handicrafts.

After Betty and Art left for home, we headed back to Presque Isle. We were both longing for the camp at the lake. It was an early spring and, even though the ground was still snow covered, we sat in deck chairs under the spring sun, trying to find peace, remembering Carol, forever our dear, little girl.

Skiing with little Carol.

Carol with Betty and Art.

Carol and Jerry.

Chapter 17

Family, Friends and Fiddleheads

I like to have young people around me. That was one of the joys of my first lakeside cottage back in Kamloops and I looked forward to being part of Ted's family when I married him. I pictured the whole family around the dinner table at Christmas, watching Ted carve the turkey. I saw us all at the cottage, enjoying a barbecue after a day of swimming and canoeing. To this day I always keep the cookie jar filled with chocolate chip cookies, a habit I started when I married Ted. However, stepping into the role of stepmother to Ted's family was not easy. While both his mother and his daughters Eileen and Bobbie accepted me right from the start, there were always tensions between Barbara and me.

Ted and I helped Barbara's husband Joe through college. Ted always expected that Joe would join him in the pharmacy business but instead, Joe bought the only other drugstore in Presque Isle, which meant he was in direct competition with Ted, who was hurt by this.

I thought things were, if not overly affectionate between Barbara and me, at least friendly. When I met her the first time, she was wearing a gorgeous buttercup yellow dress. I told her she looked gorgeous and she replied, "My mother would never have told me that."

Perhaps she resented the trips that Ted and I were often taking, and the new house and the cottage. It might have been her loyalty to her mother. Who knows what causes bad feelings in families? I regretted the fact that our relationship was no better, but I knew Ted was happy and people often told me what a difference they could see in Ted since our marriage. I remembered all the children and grandchildren with gifts on their birthdays, Christmas and special occasions. We always brought gifts home from our holidays for everyone. The family was always welcome in our home and all of them came to the cottage regularly.

One summer, our nephew Keath, Carol's brother, stayed with us for six weeks. We took him up to the cottage, went fishing and taught him to canoe. He was just sixteen that year, growing into a tall young man, looking much like his father, Gordon. It was hard to believe that both Gordon and Carol were now gone.

Just as we had done with Sean, we took Keath up to Quebec and gave him what by now was becoming our standard tour of the province. While we were staying in Montreal we took him to an elegant restaurant. He was not wearing a tie, so the mâitre d' loaned him one. He said he would never forget that night!

After he left, we slipped into our usual routine; golf

up in Amherst, Nova Scotia, at the camp for the beautiful early fall days, and down to Florida in the New Year. That summer, the family was growing so much, we decided to put bunks in the boathouse at the lake. How the grandchildren loved that boathouse! Being on their own made them feel very adventurous, but we had our safety rules. No one was allowed in the water unsupervised. There were always lots of giggles to be heard from down there at night, until, finally exhausted, the kids fell asleep.

Early in the summer we looked for fiddleheads, the curl of the ferns as they pushed their heads through the warm earth alongside the creek. Every Fourth of July we had a barbecue—salmon, new potatoes and the tender fiddleheads.

In September my brother Jack's daughter, Jacqueline Sellentin, came to live with us. Betty and I sometimes heard from Jack, who married and with three children, now lived on Texada Island. Jack's wife had died and he was not doing well. Jacqueline needed mothering so Ted and I invited her to live with us. We sent her to college that winter and the following summer she attended summer school at the University of Maine. Because I always felt the lack of formal education, I promised myself, if Betty or Jack's children needed financial help for school, I would try my level best to see they had every opportunity that Betty and I had missed.

The highlight the next winter was our Bermuda trip.

We stayed two glorious months at the lovely Castle Harbour Hotel. As always, the first thing I noticed about Bermuda, after the beaches, was the foliage. Wild Easter lilies grow everywhere and the scent is heavenly.

Scences of Bermuda.

While in Bermuda we met a couple from a very old Bermuda family, the Goslings. Mary, a nurse from Vancouver, and her girl friend, Jean, vacationed in Bermuda during the Second World War. They met their future husbands in Bermuda and just never returned home. Jean and her husband had a magnificent sailboat and often took us sailing.

One day I phoned Betty and she told me that she and Arthur were going to Hawaii for a Shriners' convention. Ted looked at me when I put down the phone. He had been listening to my conversation with Betty and said, "I guess we're off to the Islands."

We went to all the places we stayed at on our honeymoon. The Shriners had planned a busy itinerary and the days flew by. All too soon, we said goodbye to Betty and Art and a few days later we headed home to Maine.

As usual, we headed out right away to check on the cottage and open it up again. We stayed overnight and the next morning awoke to find the ground covered in snow. It was May 8.

Shortly after we came back, Ted's mother died. I mentioned earlier how fond I was of her. She was always at every family gathering and loved to come up to camp with us too. She made me feel welcome and a part of the family from the very first.

Chapter 18

South Sea Odyssey

That fall, Ted and I began to make plans for a trip to the South Seas, Australia and New Zealand. "Will there be a continent left that we haven't visited?" Ted joked. Then, for fear that I might get it into my head to take him to Antarctica, he added, "Don't answer that, hon."

I guess you could say I've always had more than a touch of wanderlust. Even now, when I no longer have a partner to share my travel adventures, I still enjoy planning a trip, either a return to a favourite spot or to someplace new. Usually now, I travel with a friend but I have been a single on at least one cruise. I just love being at sea. That said, though, cruising is no longer quite the glamorous holiday it was when Ted and I went to the Caribbean, South America, South Africa and the South Seas. Our trip to the far Pacific is a case in point.

We flew to Los Angeles and boarded the *SS Monterey* for Tahiti, New Zealand and Australia. A delightful surprise awaited us in our cabin, a beautiful bouquet from Betty and Art, wishing us bon voyage. It was not long before we had introduced ourselves to our tablemates on this star ship of the Matson Lines. Every night there was entertainment followed by dancing. During the day we swam, walked the promenade deck, played bridge, read and soaked up the sun in deck chairs. And, I worked on my latest needlework project while Ted researched our destinations. Usually someone would stop to ask me about my needlework and the ice was broken. The crew, also, made us feel pampered, turning down our beds at night, bringing morning coffee and were always willing to answer questions about the next port.

Our first stop was the beautiful island of Rotorua and the next, Papeete in Tahiti. There a fleet of canoes, each with a palm tree in the middle, and Tahitian paddlers wearing crowns and long flower leis, came to meet us. At first, we could hear them singing ever so faintly, but becoming louder and louder as they approached. I don't think I've ever experienced a lovelier welcome.

While in Papeete we visited Captain James Cook's memorial and had lunch in a restaurant where we saw the biggest cockroaches I've ever seen. In another restaurant we were served by young women, who I'm certain, were the products of liaisons between American servicemen and Tahitian women. Many of them had long blond or auburn hair and were truly beauties.

Moorea, our next stop, was almost indescribably beautiful, the tropical breezes so soft. In Bora Bora we bought canvas water shoes so we could swim near the reef without cutting our feet to shreds. The water there was so clear, we could see all the tropical fish swimming around us.

A band met us in Fiji where we took a river trip. At our destination, up river, we were treated to egg and bacon pie, or, what we call quiche.

In Auckland we hired a car and toured the North Island, where we visited the Glow-Worm-Grotto in the Waitomo Caves. A hundred thousand insect larvae, myriad specks of light, emit an eerie luminescence throughout the cave.

Criss-crossing the island, we found a good fishing lake and caught our limit of rainbow trout. That evening we lined up outside a recommended restaurant for dinner. We had no reservations but a pleasant couple ahead of us asked us to join them at their table. We got talking fishing with the restaurant owner who offered to cook the fish for our dinner. We gave a couple to our new friends and the rest to our host and the next night we returned for another delicious dinner of fried trout.

New Zealanders on both islands were very friendly but those on the South Island were considerably more British in outlook. Most of the towns have English names like Canterbury and Marlborough. As we travelled south, we saw miles and miles of sheep farms, rolling plains, rivers with fast running water and not many places to stay. We took one flight over the mountains, which they call Southern Alps, over Mount Cook and south to Milford Sound. We were told that the road into the mountain was impassable in winter because of avalanches. New Zealand reminded us of British Columbia.

We took a few days to rest in Christchurch where I discovered the Hagley Park Botanic Gardens and also visited Pollard Park in the town of Blenheim. As well as the usual massed plantings of zinnias, petunias and salvias, there was a rose garden in the park with over a thousand rose trees.

Soon we were airborne again, and off to Melbourne. I couldn't believe the garbage in the streets. It seems it was left over from something they called a walkabout, a carnival of sorts. The next day was the day of the Melbourne Cup, the famous horse race and, by then, the streets were spotless.

This city of soaring, concrete offices and modern freeways on the Yarra River also has lovely gardens and lakes shared by swans and ducks as well as many species of visiting wildlife. Melbourne was the first capital of Australia, from 1901-1927, when Canberra became the capital.

One of the best things about travelling with a Rotarian is that he can generally find a friendly fellow member almost anywhere in the world. If you are as fortunate as we were in Melbourne, you will find yourselves invited to a special event, an exclusive club, or the best restaurant in town. That is how we received an invitation to view Melbourne's racing event of the year.

"Get your best duds out, hon," said Ted. "We're off to the races."

When I stood before him the next morning and asked, "Will this do?" he replied, approvingly,

"You bet, sweetheart!"

"You look pretty swell yourself, sir!" I smiled.

He was wearing a morning suit complete with a dove grey waistcoat, an elegant tie and gloves, all courtesy of his local Rotarian friend. I was wearing a favourite white dress and navy blue coat. I wore a navy picture hat trimmed with white flowers, white gloves and pumps. We were off to the races!

When we arrived at our special box I looked around anxiously, to make sure we were suitably attired for the champagne lunch that was to follow the big race. I probably needn't have concerned myself since we found that Australians, even the cream of society, unlike Americans, didn't worry much about formalities. One woman in our box wore a complete outfit in silver lamé that wouldn't have looked out of place at a cocktail party or cabaret. Obviously we could have worn just about anything, but Ted always wanted to do the right thing when visiting a foreign country and he always appreciated the efforts I made to look my best.

As for the race and the horses? Don't ask me because I don't remember a thing except for the box lunches, the champagne, the glorious day and the fact that Ted and I were together. I still have the hat, by the way, which just goes to prove that good fashion is never out of style.

We headed up to Canberra and found a very modern city designed by Chicago architect Walter Burley Griffin. Wide circles and contoured curves give way to a long straight vista of the parliament and other government buildings. A lazy little stream, the Molonglo, passes through wide streets lined with gum trees. Several manmade lakes, parks and gardens provide a contrast to the modern buildings.

Finally, we were on our way north to Sydney, a bustling brusque city on the South Pacific. Its craggy coves, inlets and bays reminded me of Vancouver. Sydney friends we met aboard ship on our way to New Zealand were delighted to show us their beautiful city.

It was Good Friday when we arranged a game of golf with them at the Royal Sydney Golf Club. We did not pay for our game when the club members learned we were Americans. They told us that Australia was very appreciative of the role the U.S. played in World War II. I am sure the Australians felt very vulnerable, fearing invasion by the Japanese.

The Snowy Mountains were our next destination. We stayed in small huts put up by construction companies engaged in a huge hydroelectric project, diverting water from the Murray and McKenzie Rivers. We also visited an aboriginal village where we tried throwing spears and boomerangs.

Back in Sydney, there was time only to see the

movie, Dr. Zhivago and attend a concert, which featured the music from the movie. Every musician played a balalaika. There were big ones, small ones, and everything in between, and the music was simply grand! Sometimes now, when I feel a bit down and long for those days with Ted, I play the video of the movie and I'm transported back in time to that glorious concert in Melbourne.

All too soon, we were finding our sea legs again aboard the *SS Mariposa*, for the last leg of our journey on our way to Hawaii. Along the way we visited the Island of New Caledonia as well as the Solomon and Marshall Islands.

In Hawaii we visited favourite places and then flew on to Vancouver for a few days with Betty and Art. Montreal and Expo 67 was our last stop before returning home. We spent one full week visiting the many pavilions at Man and His World, thoroughly enjoying the cultural experiences with our good friends Helen and Harold Bryant. They had driven our car up to Montreal. Finally we drove home with them after more than four months of travel. We thought we had timed our homecoming perfectly. Winter would be over and the trees would be just about ready to burst into bloom. Were we wrong! On our first morning back we woke up to twelve inches of snowfall, otherwise known as spring in Maine. We were not sorry to see all the snow gone within a week, and soon we were casting our rods at Fish Lake and anticipating a summer of golf and friends visiting us at the cottage.

A new surgeon from Wales and his wife and daughter arrived in our community that summer. Howard and Anne Foy moved into the house opposite to ours and we soon discovered a mutual interest in golf, gardening and travel. Often when I saw Rachel, their sixteen-year-old daughter, I thought of my niece, Carol, at that same age, full of promise and joy, none of us knowing what lay ahead for her.

And I thought of Betty and myself when we were sixteen. What a contrast that was. Strange as it may seem though, neither Betty nor I ever really harboured any resentment about our difficult adolescent years. Whenever I see a young person who has all the advantages that love and good parents can provide, I think, "How fortunate." I know our parents never intended us to experience hard times. It was just bad luck the way things turned out.

Welcoming our new friends, the Foys, to the Presque Isle community made me feel like an old timer. When I was the new kid on the block, I knew it would take some time to find acceptance. One night we were at a barber shop quartet concert when one of the women sitting in front of me said, "Come on over for a night-cap after the concert."

"You're in now, kid. They've accepted you." Ted beamed.

The caller was Dot Hayden, one of the town's influential socialites who, with her husband, owned one of the loveliest homes in the area.

Getting to know folks in Maine meant you would be scrutinized by these New England Yankees before you received the stamp of approval. I was aware that everyone in town knew Ted and his first wife. They also knew that Ted had gone to Florida for just a week or two in the sun and stayed away for over two months while we drove across the country. There had been plenty of gossip when Ted returned home and then left soon after to visit me in Kamloops. It was fortunate that the people in Presque Isle were not malicious gossips. Ted's real friends told me later that they were so glad that Ted found someone who cared for him, after the hell he'd been through with his first wife.

I always found that playing golf well helped break the ice also, and I understand why Ted used to say that a lot of business gets done on the golf course. Golf broke the ice when Ted and I met down in Florida. One of the first things he asked me was "You don't happen to have your clubs with you, do you?" I thanked all my lucky stars and fairy godmothers rolled into one that Uncle Ben said, before we left Kamloops, "I will bring your clubs, Margaret, when I come on the train. We're bound to find some good courses."

Talk about prophetic! Sometimes I think Uncle Ben was the fairy godfather who became my guardian angel.

Chapter 19

The Far East

The next fall I went back to Expo '67 in Montreal, with Betty and Art. There were still many things to see at the World's Fair and I enjoyed the second visit just as much as the first. We also visited Quebec City before returning to Presque Isle where we had a big party for them so they could meet the many new friends I had made in the community.

We took Betty and Art bird hunting that fall and had a big Canadian Thanksgiving dinner for them before driving them up to Montreal for their return to B.C.

When we returned to Presque Isle we found an invitation waiting for us to sail on a freighter to the Orient. The American President Line's *SS Grant* would be making her maiden voyage from San Francisco, bound for the Far East, just after Christmas. Would we like to be aboard?

"You sure don't spend much time at home," was a comment from our laconic neighbours in Maine. And it was true. Not even a year had passed before we were packing our suitcases again, flying to San Francisco to stay with Ted's cousin, Eleanor Barker, a well known portrait painter, before leaving for points east. Our departure was delayed and we ended up staying at the Fairmont Hotel before our ship was ready to receive its first passengers.

Another question might also have been "Are you leaving anything at home?" In fact, in those days, travelling by ship, there were no real baggage restrictions, so we did take everything we thought we might need in the weeks ahead. Of course, there were always the challenges of transporting our luggage from airport to ship and finding space in our cabin for everything.

Finally the freighter was ready to sail and we went aboard the afternoon before our departure, taking Eleanor and her sister with us. They were suitably impressed with our quarters, comfortable beds and cozy chairs as well as a state of the art bathroom with tub and shower. When we toured the ship, looking in the dining room we saw our names on place cards at the captain's table, together with another couple from Grosse Point, Michigan, Dr. Floyd Straith and his wife, Marion. They had spotted us when we boarded and requested that we be seated with them. They were delightful companions right through the trip. Floyd was related to the Straith family, owners of well-known clothing stores in Vancouver and Victoria.

As we sailed from San Francisco Bay on a Sunday morning, an armada of small pleasure craft accompanied us. Our first destination, as we passed under the famous Golden Gate Bridge, was Hawaii.

As we sat down to breakfast one morning we noticed that the ship was eerily quiet. There was no sound from one of the ship's brand new engines. The captain informed us that it had broken down. We were soon underway again but travelling very slowly. Just before dinner that day, we hit a violent storm. We were seated at the table. Fortunately both Ted and I rarely succumbed to seasickness. Suddenly the captain shouted, "Get under the table!"

Believe me, we obeyed his order promptly and just in time to avoid being hit by flying glasses and pieces of silver.

Early on the morning of our arrival we learned that Duke Kahanamoku had died. This was the first and only time I ever heard sad Island music, such a contrast to the bright and energetic music we had come to expect in Hawaii. Kahanamoku was a world famous swimmer and Hawaiian businessman, much loved by Islanders. Ted met him once at a Rotary function and was saddened by the news.

Engine work completed, we sailed from Hawaii for the Far East.

The day before we arrived in Japan, the captain took us down in the hold to see the ship's strange cargo, millions of dollars worth of gold bricks encased in grease cans. The gold was from South Africa and the Mounties had followed it across Canada and down the West Coast to San Francisco where it was loaded onto our *SS Grant.* They wanted to nab the people to whom it was being shipped so, instead of arriving at the usual place in Yokohama, we were diverted to a military area where the people expecting the gold would be arrested. We had to wait until we rejoined the ship in ten days before we learned the rest of the gold story.

Ted and I were incredulous. You might say this was the sequel to the Edward and Gillian story. Gold smuggling just seemed to follow us everywhere we went!

Tour guides met us in Yokohama. As we stood at the deck rail we noticed that, unlike San Francisco, where we were surrounded by pleasure craft, here in Yokohama, the harbour was full of fishing and working boats.

We were soon on a train bound for Tokyo where Ted was anticipating a chance to sample the wonderful milk-fed beef. As usual he had done his homework before the trip and knew that the famous Kobe cattle were also massaged to ensure their meat would be tender. The beef was supposed to be the best in the world. It was true. The meat was so tender you could cut it with a fork, but it was so expensive most people could rarely enjoy it. I was already a fan of tempura, bite sized vegetables deep-fried in the lightest batter I had ever tasted.

Ted reminded me that we couldn't leave the busy and crowded capital city without hearing it's renowned all-girl orchestra. Young women, all dressed in long, pale blue silk gowns played western classical and romantic music. We also spent a night at the opera. Although the Japanese have produced many world class musicians in the western tradition, they have maintained their musical heritage as well. We attended a traditional Japanese opera; the performers attired in rich silk kimonos, the women wearing high headdresses and all with white painted faces.

Ted was already looking forward to a ride on the famous Bullet Train to Kyoto and the Imperial Palace. As we boarded the train he reminded me, "Get ready for a spectacular view of Mount Fuji!" The train slowed as we saw it, enabling all the photographers on the train a never-to-be forgotten opportunity to catch the snow capped mountain on film.

Kyoto, was the imperial capital of Japan for nearly 1,000 years. It was a culture that bequeathed a wealth of magnificent architecture of temples and palaces in an elegant ancient city. Modelled on the ancient Chinese capital of Ch'ang (now Xian), its chequerboard layout is an early example of the art of town planning. The Golden Pavilion was truly magnificent. When I saw a lovely hand woven picture of it, I knew that would be my souvenir of this magical place. This handiwork was so delicate that it was necessary to file the fingernails of the men who did it. Their fingernails looked just like combs, threaded with soft and subtle shades of blue, white, taupe and gold which they used to make each picture. The picture, the Golden Pavilion reflected in the quiet water beside which it stands, hangs on the wall of my house and I often stop to feel its cool, reflective mood.

When I moved into my present home, I planned a small water garden with a tiny pagoda. It is a place for quiet reflection, something every garden should have. Kyoto is still the spiritual and cultural heart of Japan.

We also toured the ancient city of Nara, an ancient Japanese capital, (which was the centre of Buddhism). Japan's oldest temple and the oldest wooden structure is the Horiuji with its great statue of the Buddha himself.

Ten days after we left it in Tokyo, we rejoined the *SS Grant* in Osaka, eager for the next instalment of the gold brick story. In Osaka, an industrial and commercial hub, we toured the ancient palaces and then were off across the Sea of Japan to Korea. In Pusan we saw half a dozen ambulances taking wounded soldiers from a troop ship to hospital. Somehow we had forgotten there was a war in Vietnam and it was my first and only glimpse of war.

Our ship was next bound for Hong Kong where Captain Bowl had arranged for us to stay at the Mandarin Hotel, Hong Kong's best hotel at that time. As we sailed into the harbour we again thought of the contrast between our homeport, San Francisco, and this harbour, bustling with small boats. We were soon engulfed by floating hawkers, selling everything from trinkets and clothes to baby chicks from their junks and sampans. Shouts and calls from all sides filled the air as well as the gobbling, quacking and cheeping of birds.

In Hong Kong, we were looking forward to meeting my old friend, Esther Gordon's son Barry and his wife, Carol. On the phone from our hotel, Carol told us she never knew when Barry, a Green Beret, might be back in town, but she invited me up to their apartment and showed me the view of the city from her balcony forty storeys above the harbour. Her table was always set for two, awaiting Barry's safe return from the war in Vietnam. Perhaps this was her way of dealing with the fears and worries associated with being a military wife.

Meanwhile, Ted attended a Rotary meeting. He was always interested in meeting fellow members, everywhere we went, and one of the many good things about Rotary International was that he could find Rotarians almost everywhere.

Carol also took us to a horse race. We had some important business to do in Hong Kong. Our next stop would be Cambodia. The war there made it off limits to Americans and if we wanted to see Angkor Wat, we would need to visit the British Embassy to obtain visas. As a Canadian, I had a visa and Ted, as my husband, was also eligible for one. They were very kind in the embassy and gave us each visas for six months.

After a lovely farewell dinner at the Meridian we said our goodbyes to Carol, our Captain and the Straiths and prepared to fly out of Hong Kong to Bangkok. After this leg of our journey, in three or four weeks, we would be joining the *SS Morrow*. We would see the Straiths in Florida the following winter.

Ted, Captain Boul, Margaret and the Straiths in Hong Kong.

Bangkok, with its many temples, was a lovely city. Although our hotel, the Erewan, the highest building in the city, had magnificent views, we were not prepared for small lizards scampering up our bedroom walls like miniature leaf shadows. Our boatman took us on the many canals, or khlongs, that give Bangkok its reputation as the Venice of the east. From its floating markets, noisy vendors tempted us with peppers, mangoes, melons and oranges as well as hats and souvenirs.

The Thai people are the friendliest we met anywhere on our trip. As Buddhists, they embody the serenity we associate with this philosophy. Their Emerald Buddha is one of the 'must sees' in the country. Our tour guide took us out in the forest to seek the now forbidden elephant logging, before leading us on a pleasant trip up the Chao Phraya River to view the King and Queen's dragon-headed boats. The whole river bustled with activity as we moved on to see the Temple of Dawn, the Wat Arun, soaring above the river. It is only one of the four hundred or so wats or temples in the city.

Reluctantly leaving the hospitable Thais behind, we arrived in Phnom Penh, the city of wide streets in the formerly French-held Cambodia. We travelled up the Mekong to a crocodile and snake farm and, before we knew it, a little girl had draped a docile anaconda around Ted's shoulders. When she tried to drape another over me, I screamed, "No, no!"

That night, after a lovely dinner in a French restaurant, I was very sick. Whether it was the wine—Ted sent his back untouched although I drank mine—or the thought of the snake, which just wouldn't go away, I don't know. Perhaps it was a bit of both.

The pictures I had seen of Angkor Wat didn't prepare us for actually being there, climbing the same steps built for the visit of Jacqueline Kennedy. All around us were temple ruins. It was a beautiful scene, but I couldn't concentrate very well because I needed to go to the bathroom and, as there wasn't one, I had to discreetly step into the ruins.

Just as I was mid-stream, I glanced down and saw a very small snake at my feet. It was spitting at me. I finished and pulled up my pants in such a hurry that I ripped a seam. Never mind. They were a favourite pair but I wasn't going to stay there one second longer than necessary.

Angkor Wat, surrounded by the trees they call 'cheese trees' because their roots look like wedges of cheese, was completed in one generation, in the 12th century. It is a blending of Buddhist and Hindu themes portrayed in a half mile long frieze. Its huge towers are lotus buds, the symbol of purity. Real lotus blooms above the muck and mire from which it rises. That night young girls danced in front of the main entrance, tiny moths attracted by the light, flying above their heads. Our brass rubbings from the temple often remind me of that ancient place deep in the jungle of Cambodia.

All too soon we were back in Phnom Penh, preparing to fly across Vietnam to Hong Kong. There we would meet up with the *SS Grant*, our floating home away from home, and pick up our extra clothes we left in Hong Kong.

The first thing that surprised us in Manila were the old army jeeps, painted in bright colours with scenes of the Philippine countryside, pictures of people working in the rice paddies and water buffalo. Named after Phillip II of Spain, the archipelago has more than 7,000 islands and several active volcanoes. Eight hundred species of orchids grow there, some of them very rare. The highlight of our visit was a trip on bamboo rafts up the Pampanga River to a beautiful waterfall and peaceful, fern-filled grotto.

Later after dining at the famous Manila Hotel, the captain took us to his favourite watering holes in the city, including one nightclub where we were entertained by stick dancers. Much to my surprise, I was soon on stage with the dancers. I remembered an old nursery rhyme, 'Jack be nimble, Jack be quick. Jack jump over the candle stick.'It took me just a few seconds to learn to be nimble and quick to avoid serious bruises on my ankles.

Heading out of the harbour, we were soon on our way across the South China Sea to Formosa, or Taiwan. Since our visit to Taiwan, I've heard many people say that it is not a place to visit unless you are doing business there. It was on our itinerary so we didn't have much choice. Ted had arranged to have a car meet us at Kaohsiung, near the south end of the island. Then we travelled up the island and we stopped for the night at Sun Moon Lake near Hsinchu. The next morning we drove out to have a look around and could hardly believe the number of American factories. It seemed as though every U.S. company was represented. Factory workers poured out of villages nearby to face long hours doing piecework for low wages.

After a trip to the famous marble canyon near Taipei, we rejoined our ship, setting sail for Yokohama. Once more we left the ship, this time travelling to Nikko National Park, high in the mountains, to visit the famous Tokugawa Shrine. It was a terrifying trip on a narrow road with at least thirty switchbacks.

"Keep your eyes closed, hon," Ted told me, noticing my white knuckles.

"Tell me again, Ted," I asked. "Why are we risking life and limb on this road?"

As usual, Ted had done his homework. Tokugawa Iyeyasu was the founder of the shogunate that ruled Japan from 1603-1867. His splendid mausoleum sits within a 350,000 acre park. When we finally arrived I was only too happy to take advantage of one of the park's features, a spa where a young blind woman gave me a soothing and restorative massage. She told me that many masseuses are blind. As I lay quietly and felt all my tensions leave my body, I realized that being blind perhaps enabled them to be more sensitive to the body language of their clients. "I can quite honestly say," I thanked her, "I have never had a better massage." Or needed it more, I thought to myself. Little did I know that I was going to need more than another expert massage to calm me before too many hours passed.

Once back in Tokyo our guide left us at the huge railway station to catch a train back to Yokohama. There were people everywhere and the noise was deafening. Nobody spoke English but Ted found our track and someone told us when it was time to get off the train. We arrived at our hotel and checked our one small suitcase in the lobby before going upstairs to have a pre-dinner drink. A short while later, from the window of the hotel restaurant, we could see the beckoning funnel of our ship. We would rejoin her after we enjoyed our dinner of tempura, udon and teriyaki.

"Just relax," Ted said confidently, "and enjoy the dinner and the view of the harbour."

When we went back down to the lobby to claim our suitcase, it was locked in a cupboard and no one could understand our English well enough to help us. Finally, in desperation, we went out into the street and found a policeman who was able to finally get our bag. It was getting late. Our ship was leaving at midnight and it was now 10:30. Then, when we found a taxi to take us to our ship, the driver couldn't understand where we wanted to go. He drove us all around the harbour before Ted eventually managed to persuade him to take us to the port agent. By the time we found our ship, I was a nervous wreck. Ted left the ship again, for a flying trip to a local shopping mall, or Motomachi, to buy flowers, fruit, candy and nuts for our trip home. As lovely as these were, I worried all the time he was gone, for fear that he might not make it back in time for our departure. I had visions of standing on the deck, weeping and waving to him back on the dock, arms filled with treats he had gone to buy for me.

It was a beautiful day in May when we sailed back into San Francisco, not a cloud in sky and no sign of fog in the bay. Eleanor Barker greeted us as we walked down the gangplank. After a few days at her place, we flew home to Maine. We had been gone four months.

Chapter 20

Mexico

Maine was enjoying an early spring that year and soon we were back in the usual routine, time at the cottage and a fishing trip or two to Fish Lake.

There is always work to do when you have a cottage as well as a house in town, but I loved gardening and enjoyed the time I spent getting things ready for guests. In between times, Ted and I both played golf and that year we went, as usual, to the annual Maritime Seniors Golf tournament. This year we went on to Prince Edward Island, where one of the local courses is right next to the Anne of Green Gables house. I was sorry that Betty and I had never read the 'Anne' books when we were growing up because Anne would have delighted us. Like her, we were orphans, too. I suppose Mrs. Archibald was my Marilla, but of course, Mrs. Archibald was never so stern. Perhaps Uncle Ben was my Matthew.

When we returned home, I discovered an unusual lump on my left side. Without telling Ted, I made an appointment to see our G.P. He saw me right away, and that evening, as we were having dinner with our friends, the Foys, the phone rang. It was the doctor. He wanted me in the hospital the very next day. I put down the phone, trying to mask my concern from Ted and our guests.

Fortunately I was left little time to worry about myself. Nevertheless, I worried plenty in the next few hours. I hardly slept that night, thinking about my mother and stepmother. Both had died so young. How must they have felt, I wondered, knowing so little time was left to them? My birth mother was perhaps spared such an agonizing time, most likely delirious with influenza. Quite likely she never knew she was gravely ill. But my stepmother knew she was dying, and I had heard how angry she was, lashing out at my father. At the time perhaps, I was more afraid for us, wondering how we would cope without her, than sympathetic to what was happening to her. How would I deal with a terminal illness? I had always been in perfect health, had more than enough energy to run my own business, look after two houses, cook, sew, play golf, fish and entertain friends and family at home and at the lake. I couldn't believe this was happening to me. Finally, unable to sleep, I got up and went out to the kitchen to warm some milk and calm my thoughts. Little André was soon at my feet, resting his nose on my slippers.

As I sat at the table by the window, trying to reassure myself just looking out at the ordinariness of my garden in the moonlight, I heard Ted behind me. After our guests left that evening I told him about the surgery scheduled the next day. It was a shock to him because I had not told him about the lump. Although neither of us wanted to look ahead to what might be, each of us wanted to comfort the other.

"Whatever happens, hon," Ted said, "We're in this together."

Our friend, Dr. Foy, performed the operation himself. When I awoke in the recovery room, Ted was there, holding my hand, trying to get through to my still groggy brain that the tumour was benign. Ted lost no time in filling my hospital room with flowers and he visited twice a day. The nurses teased us, calling us the lovebirds.

After a two-week stay in the hospital, unheard of in this time of cutbacks, I was home and on the mend. Eleanor Barker and her sister arrived in Presque Isle unexpectedly for the funeral of Ted's cousin. This somewhat interrupted my convalescence but Eleanor had been so good to us before and after our trip to the Orient, I was glad to have them stay, and glad of their company. I lost quite a bit of weight, but by Christmas time I was feeling well enough to take part in all the seasonal festivities in our small town. That was the last time, though, that I took my good health for granted. From then on I remembered each morning to stop a moment and give thanks.

Christmas meant parties and usually snow. We always carried our shoes in elegant bags as we walked through the snow in our boots. Everyone had a mat at the door for the snowy boots, replaced by high heels.

We all dressed up for the cocktail parties and usually someone threw an event at the local hotel. Ted loved me to dress up and always told me how proud he was of me. "You're pretty good looking yourself," I would tell him. And he was. He had the nicest smile of anyone I've ever known. It was just a wee bit shy and made him look very vulnerable and appealing. I often wondered what had gone wrong with his first marriage. He was so loving and caring, I just wanted to love him and care for him and never let him be hurt by anyone again.

That Christmas I gave him a book on the archaeology of Mexico and was not surprised when he suggested that we head down to Florida and fly to the Yucatan Peninsula to see the ancient Mayan ruins. I knew he'd be a first class guide for me because, as usual, he'd be off to the library for more books on the ancient civilizations of Mexico. Soon our excellent travel agent in Boston had a trip all arranged and we were off again, this time to Chichen Itza.

Chichen Itza is the site of the ruins of a Mayan city, which was an important capital between the 10th and 12th centuries. The architecture reflects both the Mayan culture and that of the Toltecs, who later invaded central Mexico.

"This well," Ted explained, "was the site of sacrifices to the rain god."

"Human sacrifices?" I asked tentatively.

"That's right," he replied. "Humans, even young women and babies. People have lived in this area since 650 B.C.,"he continued, "these ancient people had sophisticated knowledge of the solar system, in particular the cycles of the planet Venus." In the Temple of the Seven Dolls he showed me an inner chamber with windows positioned to show solar alignments.

He was eager to visit Izamal, one of the Yucatan's largest pyramids, a great religious centre and pilgrimage site before the Spanish conquest.

It was very hot and humid and we were glad we were both in good shape for all the walking and climbing involved as we learned more about the Mayan culture. We travelled everywhere by bus with all the locals, adults and kids plus chickens, and the odd goat, being bounced every which ways on roads that were rough and narrow. It was fun but, returning hot and tired at the end of the day, we looked forward to a refreshing swim in the hotel pool.

Guatemala was our next destination. Ted knew that I was very nervous about flying anywhere in Central America following the hijacking of a plane out of Miami, but he felt we were in no danger. Just the same, I was very relieved when we landed outside Guatemala City bound for the town of Chimaltenango. Soon we found ourselves in a beautiful old church; its walls blackened by centuries of smoke and soot from the wax tapers offered in prayer to the Virgin and saints. Perhaps someone asked for a child to be healed, an old person to be spared the pain of a worn out body, the successful harvesting of a crop, the return of a brother, husband or father. It was not hard to understand that the people worshipping in this sanctuary had incorporated some of their beliefs from before the coming of Christianity, into the faith of the 'Old World'. This church included an interesting museum filled with jade and potsherds dug up from graves nearby at Utatlan, which was the most powerful city of the Mayan highlands before the Spanish razed it in 1524.

Emerging from the cool dark church, we were delighted to discover it was market day at Chimaltenango. There were wonderful things to see and buy, weaving, pottery and jewellery, flat breads, vegetables and fruit and even a woman selling a litter of baby pigs! We watched a woman dicker for the piglets and later passed her, on the road to her home up in the mountains, leading them each by its own little rope.

All too soon for me, we were in the air heading for Tikal which was high on Ted's list of sights. I could easily understand why Ted was so eager to see ancient places but I was delighted to spot a quetzal bird, a regal bird with plumage as bright at Joseph's overcoat, and a lovely long tail.

While we were visiting ancient, historic Tikal, we were reminded that, in these days, you are never very far from modern technology. We watched as an old cargo plane landed, bringing a movie crew and a group of pretty young girls in colourful Mayan costumes.

The next morning we were on our way on just such an old cargo plane; one with very few seats, the passenger space filled with full bags of chicle, from which chewing gum is made. Adventurous Ted sat quite happily on the floor while I sat on one of the few seats. We soon understood that there was a problem. The pilot couldn't retract the landing wheels and in the end, we flew over the jungle with the wheels down. By the time we landed I felt so filthy all I could think of was getting into a bath.

Ted got cleaned up first and then I got into the bathtub with all our dirty clothes. By this time there was just the merest trickle of water from the tap. Ted, realizing that I was about ready to snap, left hurriedly in search of a bottle of scotch. When he returned I asked, "OK, Tarzan. Do you expect me to drink it or wash in it?"

The next day we left for Copán on an even crazier trip. A private plane took us to Tegucigalpa, the capital of Honduras, where we went through customs and then flew back to Copán.

Our last stop was Mexico City. Finally, a good hotel, clean clothes and a lovely dinner in a beautiful restaurant on a park like estate, Chapultepec.

"Tomorrow," Ted told me, "We are going to the Pyramid of the Moon." He explained that, although the site was discovered in 1910, it wasn't until 1960 that the American archaeologist René Miller and his crew actually charted the eight square miles of temples, apartments and workshops of the Pyramids of the Sun and the Moon.

The next morning Ted and I began our climb to the top of the Pyramid of the Moon. In the end, Ted went right up to the top, while I stopped just before reaching it. Mexico City's high altitude affected me and I think I was just plain tired at the end of this trip. Besides, we had tickets to the famous Ballet Folklorico that evening and I didn't want to miss that. This time, Ted had energy enough for both of us.

The dancers were wonderful, the girls in beautiful, very full-skirted white dresses. The next day we were off again to see Popocatepetl and its sister volcano, Ixtaccihuatl and then flew to Cuernavaca where I recognized, at once, among the many tropical flowering trees, the beautiful jacarandas, just like the ones in Pretoria on our African trip. As I am writing this I pause to remember the delicately handcrafted silver and turquoise jewellery we purchased in one of Taxcos cobbled streets. I'm wearing a bracelet Ted bought for me there, and I still have the cufflinks I bought for him.

Acapulco was hot but the windows of our hotel room opened out onto the bay. We spent most of our time in the water but met an American couple with a car who invited us for a drive to see the cliff divers and some of the other sights in the area. They became good friends and later visited us in Maine and Palm Desert. When it was time for us to leave Acapulco, they drove us to the airport.

Betty and Art were waiting for us in Palm Springs when we flew home to Los Angeles. They had rented a house with a pool for a month and we were looking forward to finally staying put, soaking up the sun and just taking it easy. The desert was blooming with flowers. Travel gives you a new lease on life but it can be exhausting. We were well rested, though, when we left the desert for Miami and the drive up the coast, and at last, home to Maine.

Chapter 21

Florida and Foreign Countries

That summer and fall flew by with time at the cottage, swimming, fishing, golfing and hunting. When it came time to turn off the water and close up the cottage, we looked at each other and wondered where the days had gone. We loved Maine but I found the winters long and cold. We felt we were making the right decision when we bought a mobile home on the West Coast of Florida. Ted's family were scattered, and with his mother gone, there was no reason not to go south and enjoy the sunshine, swimming and golf during the months it was cold and dreary up north. Our year was beginning to take shape; Florida after Christmas, some travel in the winter, back home to Maine for the cottage months and finally, the fall and Christmas in Presque Isle.

The doublewide mobile home at Japanese Gardens, in Florida, had two bedrooms and two bathrooms. I was busy furnishing it and then we joined the local golf club. Ted's new toy was an electric golf cart. Several people we knew in Maine were down there and we also made many new friends once we joined the golf club.

The winter went by way too fast and soon we were

heading north, stopping in Williamsburg, Virginia, this time. It was strange to think that my father had left England for the New World almost three hundred years after the settling of this area. Ted was fascinated with the apothecary shop. Many of the remedies commonly used in these first settlements on the eastern seaboard are still considered quite useful today.

We may have been enjoying the sand and sun down in Florida but we knew at once, just as soon as we saw the cottage, that the winter had been a harsh one at home and that there had been some very heavy snowfalls. Snow was still piled up around the door and in the driveway, five feet of it. A week later it was all gone and before many days passed, the family was calling to arrange camp time for the summer. Ted's daughter, Eileen, was attending summer school that year, taking courses in teaching, and asked us if we would have the boys at the cottage during the time she would be studying. I really enjoyed having them. It was almost like having my own children.

I suppose the one serious disagreement Ted and I had in our marriage was about children of our own. It was on our honeymoon in Hawaii. I wanted children and was still young enough to have them when Ted and I first met, while Ted's children were adults by then.

"I don't want any more children, hon," he reasoned with me. "I've already got a family and three kids are enough." I could see that he'd made up his mind and he could see how disappointed I was. I watched Betty's children when they were little but only longed to be a mother myself when I fell in love with Ted.

"Please, Ted," I said. "I want to have at least one child with you."

The next day he said, "I can see how much it means to you, Margaret and I don't want this to come between us. If you really want a baby that much, well OK."

It was so strange, a soon as he said that, I loved him even more and I decided to respect his wishes. For a long time after, whenever I saw a new born, I felt wistful but not full of regrets. Ted and I had a wonderful life together.

Eileen brought Richard, 13, and Robbie, 11, in August and we told them we were off on a car trip to a 'foreign' country—Canada! We went down the Saint Lawrence River to Quebec. They were really sure it was a genuinely foreign country when they heard people speaking French. We made the travelling fun by playing games in the car and singing French songs such as Frère Jacques and Alouette. They were super kids and enjoyed the experience thoroughly. We visited a typical French Canadian homestead where the woman of the house baked bread in an outdoor oven. We also bought some woodcarvings for their mom and dad.

The biggest thrill for the boys was our stop in Ottawa. After seeing the Parliament Buildings, they met our Prime Minister, Pierre Elliot Trudeau. He shook their hands and

I was able to get a snapshot of the three of them. He seemed genuinely interested in them and I thought what a good father he would make. And of course, he was a good father a few years later, to three boys of his own. I was terribly sad when his son, Michel, died in an avalanche a few years ago. When I watched Trudeau's very moving funeral last year I wished I could tell his sons about meeting their father and how kind he was to Richard and Robbie.

They were thrilled, too, to have their photos taken standing beside a scarlet-coated Mountie!

We took the boys home by way of a boat trip through the Thousand Islands and returned home over the International Bridge to New York to spend a week at the cottage with their parents. A big birthday party for Richard capped the vacation and Eileen and Chuck thanked us for making the summer so much fun. Eileen said the boys talked about the holiday for years after.

"It was the best vacation we ever had," they said. "And we really were in a foreign country. We crossed an international bridge."

It was fun for Ted and I, too, of course. I was a young grandmother and found that was a role I enjoyed, even if I never had children of my own. Now, I have another set of great grandchildren. They often come over for an afternoon's swimming in my pool and know that the cookie jar will always be filled with their favourite chocolate chip cookies.

Once Ted and I were on our own again, it was time for the Maritime Seniors' golf tournament. We always took the opportunity after the tournament to see a bit more of the countryside. That year as usual, we had a stateroom on the Digby ferry, where some of our friends gathered to party and visit. I wanted to see Lunenburg and Peggy's Cove and, for the first time, I visited Halifax. I thought of my stepmother's stories about the terrible Halifax explosion. She also loved the story of the Acadians and once read us Longfellow's poem about the young Evangeline and her separation from her lover.

Back home again, it was time for another traditional event, our annual picnic at the cottage for the drug store employees. They all looked forward to this day at the lake. It was Ted's way of thanking them for doing such a fine job running the store while we were away travelling. They took care of everything. The business had been Ted's father's and was an institution in the town for many years. When his son-in-law, Joe bought the store across the street, everyone felt he had been unwise as well as ungrateful to Ted, who helped him get his education. We wondered if Joe expected Ted to close his store and give all the business to him, but Ted was loyal to the people who worked for him and knew they would be out of work if he did that.

Presque Isle was a small town where everybody knew everyone else. People watched me closely before they accepted me into the community. That was nothing new. The same thing happened when Jack and I moved to

Kamloops. And, you can bet that tongues wagged in that small community over my relationship with Uncle Ben, my friendship with Earl and with the prominent lawyer, Davie Fulton. By the time I finally got my divorce from Jack, I knew who my real friends were and I said to heck with the rest.

That year, when we arrived in Florida, Ted said one morning at breakfast, "I guess I'm retired, now. I'm so busy since I met you, I don't have time to work any more."

When we left Presque Isle that year a young Fullbright scholar, Dennis Donham was our house sitter. The president of the local branch of the University of Maine asked if the young man could stay in our house while we were in Florida. Dennis was newly in charge of admissions and delighted to have the house. It was the beginning of a lifelong friendship.

It was certainly true that we kept busy at Englewood. Every week there was a potluck picnic in the community hall. Everyone brought a favourite dish and after a scrumptious meal, there was always dancing. The golf club had ladies' day every Tuesday and a social programme that included bridge tournaments at other clubs. Englewood has a beautiful, long white sandy beach and Ted and I spent time alone, walking the beach and collecting shells and sharks teeth. I was the collector; Ted the one with the pockets. "What are you going to do with all these shells, hon?" he asked, good-naturedly.

And, of course, it was not long before the family were coming down to Florida to spend a few beach days, soaking up the sun before returning to those harsh winters up north.

After the first winter in Florida, we started taking side trips within the state to get to know our second home better. We loved the orange groves and learned that Florida also grew sugar cane. With proud Seminole Indians as our guides, we took a trip through the Everglades in an airboat. Suddenly beautiful birds would fly up in our path, magnificent blue herons and egrets. Ever since we had started going south, each spring when we left for Maine, we returned home by a new route.

"This will be a pleasant way for you to learn the early history of the United States," Ted told me. He was always so good about taking side trips on our way up and down the coast, eager to show me something new, or old, about his country. We never worried if we took extra time and this made our trips so much more enjoyable.

It never ceased to amaze me how Ted and I fell into each other's routines so easily and how alike we were in our tastes. When I hear people talk about soul mates these days, I know that was what we were.

I mentioned earlier that, when we were on the road, we started each day with breakfast in our motel room. I always made a picnic lunch of sandwiches and fresh fruit and we usually stopped midmorning for coffee and something sweet, like a doughnut or a muffin. We ate our lunch at one of the rest stops off the highway. We stopped early enough in the afternoon to relax before finding a place for an early dinner. We both loved a good book and loved to settle in early enough for a good read before turning out the light. Ted always kissed me, last thing. "Good night, sweetheart," he'd say. I can hear his voice even now, thirty years later.

Once back in Presque Isle, we'd open the cottage, get the garden in shape and start to prepare for the first visitors. Looking back on that time, I wonder how we did so much. We were never bored.

In Maine we were able to return the hospitality shown to us when we travelled abroad. A good friend from Sydney Australia, Kathleen York, came one year. Another friend from Acapulco came and some friends from England, as well. When Ted and I were first married, I thought that Presque Isle was off the beaten track, but many friends found their way to our lakeside retreat. By now we had a powerboat and water skis for the young people and canoes and rowboats for those who wanted a quieter time or wanted to fish.

One year the Massachusetts College of Pharmacy had a fortieth reunion in Boston. It was all good fun and Ted enjoyed seeing his old chums after all those years. There was one little cloud in the sky, though. One of the men wanted Ted to accompany him to Africa in search of new drugs. I must admit, I didn't want him to go. We had never been apart, although, of course we did many things independently of each other, such as golf tournaments. We always made time for each other but also allowed each other time alone.

In the end, Ted didn't go off to Africa. Instead, we planned a trip to Malaga, on the Costa del Sol in Spain. Our friends, the Foys decided to come with us. The weather was too cool to enjoy the laid back beach life on the Spanish coast when we arrived so we took some tours and also flew to Tangiers. I was fascinated by the Moroccan architecture with its keyhole doors and beautiful cool tiles. One night we went to a nightclub where we sat cross-legged on cushions and were entertained by some beautiful belly dancers in exotic costumes. The next day we drove along the coast. We were distressed by the poverty we saw. There were people begging at every village and I wished I could take some of the beautiful brown-eyed children home with me.

Back in Spain the weather improved and we able to take it easy around the hotel pool. All too soon, the holiday was over and we were on our way home.

Alhambra Palace, Granada, Spain.

Chapter 22
England Again

Any seasoned traveller will tell you to be prepared for surprises if you decide to go globetrotting. We'd had dinner with an African witch doctor, with a different set of fine English china at each of his many tables. We'd been asked to smuggle gold out of South Africa, met the scruffiest ship's captain you can imagine. We'd been down on the floor, under a table on a cruise ship in the middle of a storm, watching dishes and cutlery fly past, and we had seen the Queen christen a new ship, thanks to an inspector from Scotland Yard. I thought I was prepared for just about anything.

Our next trip took us to England, where a rented car was waiting for us at Heathrow. As Ted reached for his wallet, he face fell. "What could it be?" I wondered. After we were robbed in Las Vegas, we always carried traveller's cheques. Had he left them back home in Maine?

"Oh damn," he exclaimed. "I've forgotten my driver's licence!" I had mine but there was no way I would drive in England. I was sure it would be a disaster. I'm a good driver but I didn't think I could handle a left-hand drive, particularly on corners. We weren't going into the city, but even so, there was bound to be traffic on the major highways.

I paid for the car and drove away. Once out of sight of the car rental people, I handed the keys to Ted.

"Be careful, Hon," I said. Don't drive too fast or too slow. We don't want to attract the attention of the police." We were on our way to Canterbury, we thought.

Wrong. Suddenly we were in the middle of heavy traffic in London. Double-decker buses, London's famous cabs, lorries, as they like to call them, and people everywhere. Were we confused? Were we suffering from jet lag? Was I afraid? You bet!

Typical woman, I said, "Maybe we should ask one of the Bobbies."

Typical man, Ted said "No sir. Didn't you say we wanted to avoid the police?"

"I did," I replied, "but that was then and this is now and we're lost and never going to get to Canterbury or anywhere else, for that matter."

"I hope they don't put us in the slammer," Ted said as he stopped the car.

"It's called the Old Bailey, here," I answered as I got

out and approached a policeman on the corner and confessed that we were lost. Naturally, I didn't mention anything about a missing driver's licence. The police, not knowing Ted was a criminal, driving without the proper credentials, escorted us to the correct road again, headed to Canterbury. Soon we were in a very comfortable bed and breakfast. Our host had a voice box, having just had a serious throat operation. He and his wife were a dear couple and insisted, once we told them about the missing licence, that we call home and get someone there to find Ted's licence and send it by fast post.

"It sure was a stroke of luck that the police didn't ask to see your licence," I said just before falling asleep.

"Luck it was not my dear," said a drowsy Ted. "It was most definitely those big blue eyes of yours."

Canterbury was a surprise. I had seen the wonderful film, *The Lion in Winter* with Peter O'Toole and one of my favourite actresses, Katherine Hepburn, about the feud between King Henry II, the King of England and Thomas, his archbishop of Canterbury. I expected to see a cathedral in a very rural setting. Of course, it sits smack in the centre of a town straight out of the Middle Ages. Narrow streets and tiny half-timbered shops really bring those far off times alive. Hearing the choirboys in the hushed cathedral at evensong is an experience I will never forget.

I was overawed by the stained glass windows, amazed at the craftsmanship of the glaziers in those long ago times.

We were among the very few tourists visiting that day and had the good fortune of having as our guide, the cathedral's verger. In earlier times, he explained, it would be his job to clear the cathedral of the many folk who used the church as a community centre. He would walk through, holding his staff with its cross on high, warning merchants, gossiping townsfolk, farmers with animals in tow, children and dogs, to clear the way for the clergy who were about to hold one of the many services of the day.

We stood before the place where Henry II's henchmen murdered Thomas à Becket. If ever there was a lesson to hold your tongue in the heat of the day, it was there in this beautiful cathedral.

Ted, being the law abiding soul he was, decided we would have to stay in Canterbury until his licence arrived from home. In some ways, it was a stroke of luck that we had to stay put. We were able to experience Canterbury and its surrounding countryside in a way that would have been impossible had we just spent a day there. We also took some day trips on the local buses, another chance to experience the community up close.

One day we took a bus to Dover and its white cliffs. From the ramparts of a Norman castle we could see France just 20 miles away. It was only then that I realized how vulnerable England had been, not just in the two world wars during the last century, but right back to the time of the Romans. Invaded by the Vikings, the Saxons and the Normans, they were threatened by the Spanish and then the French under Napoleon. I now understood why the English idolized their seafaring heroes, Sir Francis Drake and Nelson. Hitler was just another in a long series of villains, attempting to terrorize England and its brave citizens.

Once Ted's licence arrived and we were back on the road again, I was looking forward to a drive through Kent, the garden of England. My father, of course, learned his gardening skills under the tutelage of the gardener on his father's estate. He often told us about English gardens and gardening techniques. "A garden must have good bones," he would say, meaning a good basic design is necessary before you start turning sod and planting things. "Think ahead a few years and try to see what that tiny seedling will be by then. Those hydrangeas and rhododendrons will be six feet high in a few years, casting a shade around them under which only shade-loving plants can flourish. You want roses? Then you must have light! Tulips die back after a short time. What will you plant around them to cover those browning leaves that are so unsightly? That weeping willow has roots that go deep. For all his dire warnings about willow trees, there is a beautiful one in our old garden in New Westminster, still flourishing amid the 'good bones' of his landscaping.

As usual, Ted was prepared to share the history of Great Britain with me as we drove past the fields and watery meadows of an English spring. This time, though, I knew my history, as well. I knew that Nelson had died aboard his ship and that his body had been preserved in a barrel of brandy. I knew about the Prince Regent's extravagant holiday pavilion in that graceful old city, Bath with its elegant crescents and narrow lanes. And then, there we were standing dockside at Southampton, at the very spot from which the Pilgrims set sail aboard the Mayflower bound for a new life in Plymouth, never to return to family and friends.

It was always fun travelling with Ted. He was never in too much of a hurry to window shop in antique stores or have a leisurely meal of fresh lobster or a typical English 'cream tea' of scones, clotted cream and strawberry jam. "Stay as long as you like, sweetheart," He would say. "I'm happy when I'm with you."

And often now, I think of that old song of the 1920's,

Sometimes I'm happy, Sometimes I'm blue,
My disposition depends on you.
That's how I am, so what can I do?
I'm happy, when I'm with you.

It was true for me, as well.

Chapter 23
Old 'Friends'

After Sean left to go back to Ireland, we thought we had heard the last of our Irish friends, Edward and Gillian. To our surprise they continued to send us cards at Christmas and, although we didn't want to get involved in any of Edward's schemes, we always sent a card to them.

However, a new doctor and his wife, Peggy and Bill O'Brien from Kilkenny, arrived in Presque Isle. Peggy and I shared a love of golf and we soon became good friends and golfing partners. One day I asked the couple if they, by any chance, knew Edward and Gillian. They did. Peggy said people were very suspicious of them, back home, and wondered where all their money came from. She also said the police had been checking on them for years but could never find anything criminal with which to charge them.

When we decided to visit Ireland that August we sent them a note to let them know. We arrived at Shannon airport and planned to go north, up the west coast. A friendly couple saw us looking at our road map in the town of Eames and asked if they could help us. When we told them we were looking for a place to stay, the woman turned to her hubby and asked, "Where will we send them, dearie?"

They directed us to a lovely old inn with a pub. There was a lively crowd in the pub, singing and having a good time. With the welcome they gave us, we were soon singing along, each of us with a pint of Guinness. Our first impression of Ireland was delightful. The next day, not too early, and over our jet lag, we were back on the road heading for Galway Bay. I could hear Bing Crosby crooning the beautiful lullaby, *Galway Bay*.

If you ever go across the sea to Ireland, and here we were, having done just that. I could well understand the homesickness of the thousands of Irish who were forced to leave their homeland in the terrible famine that followed the potato blight in the 1840's. Thousands, who couldn't leave, starved to death. Poverty is terrible. I've seen too much of it in my travels around the globe, in South America, Africa and the Far East, and I often wonder why, when we can do so many things with technology, we can't rid the world of the poverty that makes life, itself, a burden to so many people.

My father often read poetry to us when we were growing up. W.B. Yeats was a favourite poet. I thought of those haunting lines, *A terrible beauty,* as we drove past the stone fenced fields. Ted, of course, had done his homework and I needed no other guide through Connemara National Park and on to Dublin.

Once we settled into our room at the Sherbourne Hotel in the heart of the city, he said we must see the Book of Kells, at Trinity College. This beautifully illuminated treasure was written in the ninth century, he told me. It was a time when much of the knowledge and most of the writings of Christianity were preserved in monasteries. Cloistered scribes laboured with love to preserve and illuminate the ancient texts of the faith, at a time when men outside the cloisters had lost their respect for learning. The first thing I thought of when I saw the Book of Kells, was how much it reminded me of needlework. The detail and colours were truly inspiring. And of course, in the hands of the noblewomen of the same period, the needle arts were preserved.

The Quays and the River Liffey, Dublin, Ireland.

When I was growing up I often heard grown ups say "The devil makes work for idle hands. "I don't think either Betty or I would ever have said we were bored, because we never were. Our brother Jack, on the other hand, often looked sullen or bored. But even he would never give voice to that thought, because our parents would only too quickly respond, "Nothing to do? We'll soon give you something to fix that, young man."

Our parents expected us to help with the many chores associated with our father's business; weeding the garden, cleaning the fishponds, even, to the detriment of our health, cutting up gypsum. In the house, there was always dusting, ironing, meal preparation and washing up to be done.

Still, as I've said before, I always find a space in my life for needlework. I've done needlepoint and petit point versions of famous works of art such as *The Blue Boy* and *Pinky*, but what I like to do best are flowers. I've had a garden everywhere I've lived and love flowers of all kinds so it gives me great pleasure to embroider a rose, a daisy or a poppy. I think doing this work has made we more observant of real flowers with both their vibrant colours and their subtle shadings. It never fails to amaze me just how many shades of green there are around me. Obviously the people who design needlework kits are aware of all these complexities in nature and so I feel a kinship with someone I've never even met.

It's also amazing what a wide variety of people, both men and women, do needlework. Recently, Kaffe Facett, in England, has published several books showing many of his designs. He also encourages people to design their own projects, once asking people to picture their homes. His use of vibrant colour shows that needlework is alive and well. I believe Prince Charles also does needle work and, as well as Facett, there are other men writing about the art.

Margaret with her award-winning flowers.

As well as walking the same streets as the many famous Irish writers such as Jonathan Swift, W. B. Yeats and James Joyce, we wanted to see a play at the Abbey Theatre, where Gillian acted before she went to South America and Africa with Edward.

"Before we leave," said Ted, "I must see a hurling match." I had no idea what he was talking about but we found there was one that afternoon.

The next day we set off south to Dun Laoghaire, and then to see the beautiful Dargle Glen Gardens and the Powercourt Estate. It was late in the afternoon, as we were driving through the Wicklow Mountains, when, wouldn't you know, our rented car suddenly quit on us. We had passed a few isolated houses on the road and Ted decided to walk back to one and knock on the door. Unfortunately he was wearing a black raincoat and perhaps the people thought he was a gangster. He tried a few houses and finally a man and woman said they would call a garage for us. As dusk fell in the mountains, we waited for a tow truck. It was eerie as we waited and we were very thankful when we arrived at the next town and found a place to stay.

The next morning Ted checked on the car and found it would soon be ready for us to set off again. The night before we phoned Sean Thompson's parents. He was now living in Ontario and married, working at a heavy water plant for Ontario Hydro. His parents, who lived in Wicklow in the beautiful Glendalough Valley, rolled out the 'red carpet' for us, serving us a delicious high tea when we arrived and dinner later in the evening. Mrs. Thompson insisted that we come back the next morning for breakfast when she served us scrambled eggs and the most luscious mushrooms, which grew under a huge and ancient oak tree in their garden.

It was hard to leave that idyllic spot, especially when we were soon to meet Edward and Gillian, in Kilkenny. They had reserved a room for us at a very old hotel. Edward would be coming for us in the early afternoon.

He drove us out to their estate, Gillian's old family home with walls six feet thick. Edward had fruit trees which, as it was fall, were laden with apples and pears. He was producing root stock, small enough trees from which the fruit could be picked without climbing a ladder.

He seemed to be doing well and took us by surprise when, after dinner, he brought up the subject of gold smuggling again. He said he was very disappointed that we had not been willing to take his money to New York for him.

Edward and Gillian at their home in Ireland.

Ted was diplomatic but told Edward he was somewhat surprised that it had taken him so long to say this to us. And we left. But not before Ted said that he wondered if Edward might have been worried that we might inform the police about what Edward had asked us to do.

"You didn't seem to worry about the trouble we would have been in if we had agreed to your plan."

I guess we were very naïve. Edward was totally without scruples and was prepared to use us and compromise us in a way that might have landed us in jail. He and Gillian seemed such a nice couple when we met them in South America and we were flattered when they invited us to Africa. He was also prepared to use Sean as an accomplice, which was even worse, since Sean's future might have been very dismal. Instead of going to Ontario, he, too, might have found himself behind bars. I guess we found out the hard way that you have to be cautious when travelling.

In all fairness to Gillian and Edward, they did

show us a marvellous time and since talking to folks in Vancouver who have emigrated from South Africa, I understand that it is still hard to get money out of that country.

Sean and children.

There were so many things to see in Ireland and as well as wanting to visit the Waterford Crystal Factory we were determined to play at least one round of golf. We soon found out why the country is so green. It rained steadily as we made our way around the course at the Ring of Kerry. We even had to bend over backward and kiss the Blarney Stone in a downpour. I told Ted that he didn't need to kiss it to have the gift of eloquence bestowed upon him.

It continued to rain as we made our way to Dingle, where we knew there was a lovely hotel. There were waterfalls all along the road, spilling water everywhere and when we arrived at the hotel it was closed. There was no place else to stay. We were lucky to find a farmhouse bed and breakfast, but it was late by then and we were ravenously hungry. The dear old couple who ran the place gave us a drink and a simple supper that tasted wonderful. The next morning we had a good breakfast of ham, eggs, tomatoes, potatoes and toast with homemade jam, before setting off down the road. The farm was picture perfect, and sure enough, we had not gone far before we saw huge trucks parked at the side of the road. Someone was making a movie there.

On one of our last nights in Ireland, we stayed in a castle. The bedroom with its four poster bed and the baronial hall and dining room set with silver and crystal seemed so far removed from the modest but welcoming farmhouse bed and breakfast we enjoyed the day before. It was fun to dress up for dinner elegantly. I told Ted anyone would think he was 'to the manor born'. He really did look great in formal clothes. I mentioned earlier that he had what everyone in the business called 'the pharmacist's stoop', just ever so slightly bent over, and with his shy smile, he was hard to resist. Not that I ever tried to.

It was still raining when we headed for Shannon to fly home. On our last day in Ireland, we visited Bunratty Castle, a folk park of thatched cottages, a tavern and shops. That evening we went to a medieval banquet eaten without knives or forks. It was messy but fun. I felt like a naughty child as I gnawed on a bone and then threw it on the floor. Ale flowed freely amid laughter and Irish good spirit.

Bunratty Castle Feast.

While we were away there was an embargo on oil and a gasoline price hike. We remembered the time, back in the 1950's, that

Egypt chose to assert its sovereignty over the Suez Canal, then considered to be Great Britain's possession. War ensued. The canal remained closed for some time. As I write this, we are once again threatened by trouble in the Middle East.

That winter, 1974, we had the opportunity to rent our place in Florida and we decided, instead of going south, to return to Hawaii. Because we had a two-bedroom condo, Ted's daughter Eileen and her husband spent a couple of weeks with us, followed by my sister, Betty, and her husband, Art.

Chapter 24

Loss

When we returned home, I decided to take lessons in oil painting and continued to work at my needlepoint whenever I had a spare moment or two. Although Ted and I were away for long periods, it wasn't until 1975 that he officially retired. Now we spent Christmas and New Years down south. I was glad that we had tested the waters of our new community style of living before we made a final decision and would recommend doing that to anyone considering a major life style change. Try it out before you put too much into it. Of course, the sooner you involve yourself in a community, the sooner you'll feel a part of it. We met new friends and also knew many people from Presque Isle who were 'snowbirds' like us. The potluck dinners, golf games and bridge parties were excellent opportunities to build connections. Then, we finally decided that year to sell the cottage at the end of the summer. The grandchildren were growing up and we were spending longer periods in Florida. In fact, we began to consider building a home in Englewood.

It is always hard to give up a home when one has put so much love into it. I looked at the garden, remembering all the work I did to clear the rocks. It had been fun to furnish and decorate the cottage and to build the boathouse with all the bunks. We had many happy times to look back on. It had been a good place for us. But now, we had another project.

It wasn't long before we had an offer and a down payment for the cottage. We were planning to go back down to Florida but first, we flew out west to attend my nephew Keath's wedding. It was a lovely occasion in Betty and Art's garden. We planned to stay an extra few days with my sister and her husband after the wedding but one morning Ted told me he thought we should go home sooner. There was a lump under his arm and he wanted our friend, Dr. Foy, to have a look at it. "It's probably nothing to worry about, Hon," he said. I was worrying, though.

Dr. Foy was concerned, also, when he examined Ted. "I'd like you to see a specialist in Boston, " he told Ted. "I'll make an appointment for you right away."

It was the beginning of a nightmare. "Your husband has lung cancer," he told me. "I doubt that he has more than a few months to live. There is nothing we can do. I'm sorry."

Ted was very practical. "Northern Maine is no place for a woman on her own," he said. He insisted that we sell our beautiful home. It didn't take long to sell and with it, I foolishly sold my beautiful royal Kerman rug. I have regretted parting with it ever since, but when your life is falling apart, you don't always think things through.

Once the house was sold, we headed for Florida. Neither of us knew what was ahead but Ted insisted that we pick out plans for the new house. "If nothing else, it will give us something positive to think about," Ted told me. "Besides, Margaret," he added, "We've got to be practical. I'll have no peace of mind until I know you'll be comfortable after I've gone."

I didn't want Ted to talk this way. I couldn't believe what was happening and couldn't imagine a life without him. I was frightened and angry and, I suppose, looking back on this awful time, I must have subconsciously been taken back to the death of my parents. First my own mother, the one I had never known, then my stepmother and father. "Why me?" I thought. "Why is this happening to us when we love each other so much?"

As soon as Betty and Art heard the news, they wanted to take us to Hawaii. Ted was not yet under treatment and at this time was not in any real discomfort. Dr. Foy had no objection so off we went and stayed at a lovely new hotel, right on the beach in Honolulu.

I watched anxiously as Ted grew thinner every day. When we returned, we would fly to Florida where he would begin a course of chemotherapy that would, at best, only postpone the inevitable. As we soaked up the sun and watched the surf, Ted put on a brave front. I had a terrible ache in my heart. I couldn't bear to lose him.

Back in Maine, a friend drove our car down to

Florida. We flew down and found our friends had stocked the fridge and cupboards with all the food we'd need for a while. Ted's chemotherapy began immediately. It was pure hell. We never got home after the treatments without Ted asking me to pull over so he could get out of the car and throw up. The worst thing was to watch him suffering so much and be unable to help.

By the end of September our new house was finished. Our contractor arranged for his crew to look after all the finishing details, including the landscaping and right down to hanging our pictures. Ted came with me to choose the furniture although he was so tired he would generally find a chair in the store and would sit and wait patiently while I talked to the sales people. His chemotherapy was over and we both hoped he had bought himself a few more months.

That Christmas, 1978, was our last one together. Ted's daughters, Eileen and Bobbie came with their husbands and, for Ted's sake, we tried to make the holiday the same as always with the traditional turkey dinner and presents around the tree. It must have been a very great effort for Ted to even take part. He spent much of the day in bed and, after everyone left for home, he seemed so much worse. Betty and Art came back and by the time they arrived, he was seeing double and his skin was burned from the radiation treatments.

On one of the last days Ted left the house, Art took him to the bank where he signed all the necessary papers to put everything under our joint names. When they came home, Art went right out to the woodpile where he chopped all the wood left when the contractor cleared our lot before laying the foundations of the house. Poor Art, I think this was the only way he could deal with what was happening to Ted. The two were very close, as over the past few years we spent many holidays with Betty and Art. The two of them just seemed to hit it off right from the start. Winters in our part of Florida could be quite cold and I was grateful to Art for his wood chopping because it meant that we would have warm fires in the family room of our new house every evening. In those last few days before Betty and Art left for home, the four of us would sit in front of the fire and pretend that nothing had changed.

One day Ted said, "Hon, after I'm gone, I want you to remarry. I want to know that you'll always have someone to watch over you when I'm gone. You know, Lou's a good guy. He'd make a good companion." Lou was one of Ted's golfing buddies. He only had one lung himself and, whenever he visited, he kept telling us that Ted would recover.

However, the last thing I wanted to hear from Ted was that Lou should take his place. "I don't want anyone but you, Ted, "I told him. "Don't talk like that."

Since Ted became ill, we had many late night talks. He always said, "I'm so sorry, sweetheart. I thought we'd grow old together." I always tried to reassure him by telling him that even one year with him was worth fifty with anyone else. And I meant it.

It was obvious that Ted couldn't last much longer. Although we had nurses coming in every day and I was getting used to giving Ted his morphine injections, the doctor thought Ted should be in hospital. Getting him there was more of an ordeal than we could ever have imagined. Bobbie, Ted's daughter and her husband, Ray, came over from Pompano and helped me get Ted into the car. I drove with Ted beside me, and Ray and Bobbie sat in the back seat. We were on the highway when I saw a car approaching us but veering dangerously near the white line. As it passed us I tried to give it a wide berth when I heard a shot. It all happened so quickly. I saw a brown arm with a handgun pointing out of the front window. I heard a shot but could scarcely take in what was happening to us. The windshield shattered and there was broken glass everywhere. The bullet lodged in the dashboard. Had it been any higher I would have been hit. I must have been in such a state of shock over Ted, that I really didn't take in what had just happened, but after we saw Ted safely into his room, Bobbie and Ray asked me if I was going to report what had happened to the local police. Until then, I hadn't even considered it.

"Honestly, Margaret," Ray said, "I really think we should report it."

Reluctantly, I agreed. What happened next was even more unbelievable. The police could not have cared less.

After questioning us for what could not have been any longer than five minutes, they told me I should not have been driving in Florida with a driver's licence from Maine.

"For God's sake," Ray exclaimed. "This woman's husband is dying and we have just been shot at on the highway! Surely you've got something to say about what happened to us?"

The police didn't give a damn. And at that point I began to fall apart. From the beginning of Ted's illness, through the sale of our house and cottage in Maine and the move to Florida, knowing Ted was dying, I kept calm. But I was nearing the end of my rope. I started to shake and then to weep.

Saying, "Never mind these people, Margaret," Bobbie and Ray led me back to the car and drove me home.

A day or so later Ted's doctor called me to say that Ted could not last much longer. He knew that Ted wanted to be at home with me when the end came and so he arranged for an ambulance to bring Ted back one last time. I called Ted's brother, Bob. They had never been close and Bob said he would come in a few days. "You'd better come right away," I told him and he arrived only a few hours before Ted died in my arms.

Chapter 25
Lou

I'm eighty-four years old now. More than twenty years have passed since Ted died. I have talked to many women who have lost their husbands, and everyone tells me the same thing. Even if you know that your husband is very ill, you are never prepared for the end when it comes, because you never believe it will really happen. Ted's brother, Bob, handled all the funeral arrangements, including the notices in the papers in Florida and back in Maine. Betty came and Ted's daughters, Eileen and Bobbie were supportive. It was all a blur to me. I was numb with grief.

Ted was so well known, both in the pharmaceutical business, in Rotary International and the Shriners, that tributes and flowers poured in from all over the country. The funeral was a comfort in a way. People told me, over and over, how fortunate Ted had been to have married me and been able to start life again after those sad years with his first wife. What they didn't know was how lucky I had been to find Ted, after the misery of my first marriage. I was still relatively young and had a lot of years ahead of me without him. At first, I couldn't imagine how I was going to do it.

Betty had been through the same thing, of course, when her first husband, Gordon, died in a plane crash. I never did know how she coped with Carol's death, but I guess it was just the way we survived after both our parents died when we were teenagers. Survive we did, but I made a very bad decision to marry Jack, not because I loved him, but because I thought life with him would be better than trying to struggle along on my own. At first, life didn't seem worth living without my darling Ted. There was trouble ahead.

For a few months I drifted. Sometimes I was terribly sad and then I was angry. Why did this have to happen? What was life all about anyway? So many truly awful people went about their lives doing real harm and seemed to get away with it. I didn't want to go any place where I might see couples enjoying themselves. I didn't even want to visit old friends. But finally, I had to say to myself, "Look, Margaret, you are alone and you've got to face up to that. Ted wouldn't want you to be living like this. You've survived a lot of things, managed your own business, have a nice home and garden. Pick up those golf clubs, go out in the sunshine and get on with it."

I knew the first thing I'd have to face up to would be taking Ted's ashes back to Presque Isle. I would have to see all the places we'd both loved, one last time. The sooner the better.

I flew up to Ted's sister, Deb, in New York and then on to Presque Isle, where my dear friend Anne Foy met me. I stayed with Anne and Howard while I arranged to place Ted's ashes in the local cemetery. The problem was that Ted always thought he had a plot in the cemetery but he wasn't aware that this plot had been used for a little brother. I was able to purchase another plot nearby, and one beautiful spring day we held a committal service attended by a few close friends and family. I had to admit that a beautiful part of my life was over as I said a final goodbye to my dear Ted.

"I will always love you, Ted," I told him in the quiet moment I had alone in the cemetery.

Almost immediately I flew to Vancouver where I stayed with Betty and Art. Near the end of my visit, we took the ferry over to Vancouver Island, where we visited Long Beach on the West Coast. Something about the sea with its pounding surf and the massive old growth forest trees restored my spirit, and after visiting beautiful Butchart Gardens, I flew home to Florida. And I did feel I was going home.

I found it very hard to be alone. Caring for Ted had been the focus of my life and there was never a day when I didn't wake up to the knowledge that the day's routine was already planned. Now I had to make an effort to get up, eat breakfast and decide what to do with the day.

Lou DuBois, Ted's golfing buddy, started dropping by. Two professors in the complex, from Bates College in Maine, knew him and told me he was a smart fellow but I really knew nothing about him. Good looking, 'The Silver Fox' as we called him, had the self-confidence of a former professional baseball player. He was a good golfer also, and before long, everyone at the golf club got used to seeing us on the links together every day. Afterwards we'd eat at the club or I'd invite him back to my place for a home cooked meal. I enjoyed cooking, missed making meals for Ted and couldn't face eating alone. And, another thing women who've lost their husbands will tell you, is that one of the hardest things to get used to, after a loved one dies, is sitting by yourself at the table and wondering why you even bother cooking. Lou seemed to enjoy my company and my cooking. If we went out to eat, he always paid the bill and always seemed to have money.

There's no doubt about it, Lou was good looking and knew how to please a woman. He never told me much about his personal life, though, and I just assumed that his first marriage had not been happy. I thought he was good company and naively, I suppose, I sensed that he was not the marrying kind. That was fine with me. I just enjoyed his company and the fact that I didn't have to be alone. And let's face it. My relationship with Ted had been everything a woman could desire. He was a tender lover and I missed that and missed the cuddling that is an important part of a woman's desire. Lou was a virile man who understood women.

He took me by surprise one day, after our usual 18 holes, as we were having drinks on the club patio in the late afternoon sun. He asked me to marry him. I heard myself say yes. I wonder, now, if he was as surprised as I was. It was a foolish decision and soon after our wedding, I knew it was a mistake. I knew nothing about him. When I told Betty that I was going to marry Lou, she was dubious. "Just wait awhile, Margaret," she advised. "You know nothing about him and you might regret this."

However, Ted's children seemed happy for me and I married Lou on Dec. 8, 1979, not quite a year after Ted's death. It was a lovely affair in the local Anglican church. I wore a white lace dress and Lou looked very handsome in a white suit. Now, when I look at the pictures of our wedding, I'm surprised at how happy we looked because it didn't last.

Lou and me.

We went down to Captiva Island to stay in a time-share Ted and I owned. It is a lovely spot, very tropical and has a small golf course on which you could play if you owned a condo. We came back in time for Christmas. Bobbie and Ray came over from Pompano, where Ray had horses, and they both seemed to like Lou. He often went off to play golf with his buddies but the men, like the women members of the club, golfed together and I didn't think much about Lou going off on his own.

That next summer we spent in Florida. With fewer people around, we enjoyed the warm beaches and a relaxed life style. Lou was often out but I didn't think much about it. He said he had business to do and, since I still had no idea of his financial situation, I believed him.

We planned to go to B.C. in the fall to help Georgina and Keath put on a party for Betty and Art's 25th wedding anniversary and flew to Vancouver the middle of October.

We celebrated my birthday, first, at Harrison Hot Springs, where we spent a few days before returning for the wedding anniversary celebration at the Seymour Golf Club. Betty said she just wanted a few friends, but Georgina, her daughter in law, invited a hundred or more.

With everything ready for the party, which was to surprise both of them, we had to think of a way to get Art up to the Club. We sent Lou there to practice golf that afternoon. When it came time to leave, Betty thought we were going to a restaurant down town. Lou said he had left his wallet in a locker at the Club and said we'd have to go by there before going down town.

To say that Betty and Art were surprised to see over one hundred of their friends and family waiting for them on the steps of the club, wouldn't come close to describing it! Georgina and Keath put a huge sign out at the front of the club saying 'Happy Twenty-Five Years'. It was a terrific party and they were completely surprised. I am sure they loved every minute of it.

When Lou and I headed back to Florida, two of my good friends suggested we have lunch after our weekly round of golf. "Listen, Margaret," they said, "Quite a few of us are worried about you and we've decided we should warn you about Lou. Did you know he was living with another woman before you two got married?" Of course I didn't know. And, I didn't want to believe her.

"What's more," she continued, "we've seen him with her several times. You'd better start thinking about leaving him and also, we think you should see a lawyer right away." It seems there was a law in Florida, which forced you to divide your assets with your spouse if you had been married two years. I phoned my lawyer and he confirmed this.

"Margaret," my lawyer, who was also a good friend, said, "You'd better come down here for a chat. This Lou guy is bad news. We've been pretty worried about you ever since Ted died. We should have warned you about Lou before you married him."

I had been trying to ignore the fact that a woman phoned and asked for Lou quite regularly. She would never leave her name. Whenever I asked Lou about her, he would give me some off hand reply like "Oh, she's the wife of a fellow I used to know in Miami. I'm just a shoulder to cry one when she's miserable." At first I believed him, but as he began to be away more and more, the alarm bells began going off in my head. Lou, early in his baseball career, had adopted the lifestyle common to so many professional sportsmen. There are always women in every town and city willing either to be one night stands or hoping for a permanent relationship with men who seem glamorous and wealthy. Could I have fallen in to that trap? That thought filled me with remorse and anxiety. Thinking back to those first two years after Ted died, I realize that I was probably temporarily insane. How else can I explain my marrying Lou so soon after Ted's death? Worse was yet to come.

I went to see my lawyer and he told me that if Lou and I separated after two years of marriage, Lou would get half of everything I owned. I didn't want to confront Lou but knew I had to start to make plans to divorce him before it was too late. I felt foolish and angry with myself for being so gullible and not listening to the subtle hints about Lou. Even Betty, wanted me to wait.

"It's too soon, Margaret," she said. At least wait a year. You might be getting into something you'll live to regret."

But, of course, I hadn't listened. Looking back I can see a pattern in my relationships with men. It's a pattern that sometimes gets me into hot water to this day. I suppose after my father died, I was always looking for someone who would look after me. I don't know why exactly, because I lived independently and successfully for many years on my own. But always, during those independent years running the motel, men would be attracted to me, giving advice, smoothing the way and always telling me they wanted to look after me. Ted was a real nurturer but he could have just as easily been bad news because I really didn't know him all that well when we got married. I was lucky in love with Ted. Jack, my first husband, was abusive and Lou was another bad choice. Perhaps there's a little girl deep inside me, still saying, "Daddy, why did you leave us?" Both Betty and I had to adopt a tough attitude to survive but I think there are some men who can sense a woman's vulnerability and will take advantage of that if they can.

In the spring we drove back up to Presque Isle. Lou loved baseball and I was beginning to learn 'baseball speak'. Lou mentioned that he had an aunt living in Bangor Maine. He even knew her phone number. I remarked that he had a good mind for numbers. If you told him a phone number once, he didn't need to ask again. So I said, "Why don't we stop and see her?" He phoned her from Boston to say we would stop in.

Lou's aunt greeted me at the door while Lou took our suitcases out of our car. My heart sank as she said quietly, "He isn't any good. Did he tell you about his daughter? He is already married. He causes nothing but heartache."

On our drive to his aunt's place, Lou told me that both his aunt and her daughter were nurses who had nursed in Hawaii during the war. While we were getting acquainted and talking about the Islands, Lou decided to visit some old baseball buddies. As soon as he left, the two women wasted no time in warning me about him. They felt very sorry for me and said more than once, "Just phone if you need us and we will be right down".

In Presque Isle, I visited my old friends and played a round of golf. Lou, handsome and dressed impeccably, impressed most of my friends who thought that I was very lucky.

"You two could easily be models," several people remarked.

I learned from my parents that you don't tell your friends your troubles. However, as soon as we headed back to Florida I consulted my lawyer. He repeated his earlier warning. If a marriage lasted two years and ended in divorce in Florida, my money and property would be divided and Lou would get half of what I had. I immediately started divorce proceedings. I became afraid of him and asked him to leave. He didn't always come home anyway. Then I phoned his aunt and cousin in Bangor and they said they would be down as soon as they could arrange a flight. When I told Lou they were arriving, he wouldn't even drive up to Tampa with me to meet them. I went by myself. They were wonderful support for me. When we arrived back in Englewood, Lou had packed up all his things and was gone.

He went out to his son's in Seattle. I think I married him because I felt sorry for him. One never learns. His kind aunt and cousin went back to Maine, suggesting that I should try and get away for a while. They knew

Lou better than I did, thinking he might not step out of my life so willingly. I'm sure they were trying to warn me that Lou had a violent side to him, as well. Fortunately, I never saw that. Lou died later in Seattle.

Chapter 26
Colin

I decided to book a cruise to Alaska, stopping in Vancouver to stay with Betty and Art. It felt good to be back in B.C., leaving all the trouble with Lou behind me. I knew then and still know to this day that a cruise is just another way of escaping when life gets unbearable. If you have the money to do it, it probably beats hours on the analyst's couch. Yes, I was escaping not just from Lou, but also from the trouble I'd had trying to live alone after Ted died.

I could see the relief on both their faces when Betty and Art met me at the airport. "Thank heavens you got out of that bad marriage," Betty told me. "We were always wary of Lou, Margaret. There just seemed to be something not quite right about him. Maybe he looked just too good to be true."

I thought again about Ted. He was good looking, too, but it was the little things that weren't perfect about his looks, like his 'pharmacist's stoop' and his shy grin that melted my heart. I vowed right then, never to get seriously involved with anyone else until I knew a lot more about him.

I didn't have long to wait. Before I left Florida, Dick Strongert called me. I knew he lived in one of the local trailer parks and that he probably didn't have much money but he was another charmer, very handsome, with a real gift of the gab. He was very attentive and listened sympathetically when I told him about Ted and the mistake I had made in trusting Lou. I didn't want anything serious to develop between us but we played golf together and drove up to the beautiful Calloway Golf Course in Georgia for a tournament. This involved an overnight stay and we just naturally spent the night together. There are men around, and not just gigolos, either, who are good lovers and he was one of them.

Dick and me.

Back in Englewood, I packed to go to Vancouver and on my trip to Alaska. Dick wanted my address and phone number in Vancouver. He phoned me several times while I was at Betty and Art's place, saying he missed me and wanted me to let him know when I was returning from my cruise. When I left the cruise ship, back in Vancouver, he was there to meet me.

Betty and Art were afraid things were getting too serious between Dick and me, and thought I was being foolish when I agreed to go to Vancouver Island with him. I told them I could look after myself and, while I enjoyed Dick's companionship, I didn't want to make another mistake like the one with Lou. So, once back in Florida, I decided to go to Bermuda to stay with my friend, Jean, and give myself time to think. Dick followed me over there.

Jean didn't like him but she gave a party for me and invited Dick. After the party, while we enjoyed a late drink beside her pool, she said "Margaret, he's not for you". She said he would break my heart.

"He's a flirt, Margaret. I watched him tonight. He's just trouble."

Betty had been worried, too. She phoned me while I was at Jean's, suggesting that I bring Dick and meet them at Captiva Island in Florida. They said they were willing to withhold their opinion of Dick until they could see him again. Art didn't like him any better the second time.

He got on the line and said, "He is just after what you have and he is a smoothie. Find a way to get rid of him before you find yourself in another mess."

That night by the pool, when Jean warned me not to get involved with Dick, she asked, "What's the matter, Margaret? You've always been so level headed. It's not like you to be running around like this." That was all it took. All the tensions and sorrows of the last three years unleashed a torrent. I cried and cried and Jean just put her arms around me and waited.

"It had to come out," was all she said.

I knew my affair with Dick had to end. Betty and Art were relieved when I told him I would be going back to Vancouver for Christmas. But, I was torn. I didn't know what to do. I seemed so alone in Florida. It seemed all I did after Ted died was fly back and forth from Vancouver to Florida or go off on a cruise to get away from another man. I thought back to the time when I owned the motel and ran my own business. Sure, there were men in my life back in those days, but I was always in charge of the relationship. I was never at risk back then. I'll admit, I do like the company of men and sometimes find them easier to be with than women. Now it seemed to me that I would never have another relationship like Ted's and mine. I'd just made one mistake after another and I knew Betty and Art and Jean were not the only ones worried about me.

Christmas at their place, with all the bustling to buy gifts, decorating the tree and helping Betty with the baking could have been another sad occasion but, surprisingly, it was fun. There was a new baby in the family. Georgina and Keath's baby son, Adam was the centre of attention. He was born on September 1st, and at four months, was delightful.

Betty and Art's home was in Deep Cove, a lovely waterfront community with a small street of shops, good restaurants and a theatre and art gallery. It is also one of the destinations of the carol ships, a fleet of brightly lit small boats playing Christmas carols. The music wafts over the water to people on the shore and in homes along the waterfront. Our friends, Margie and Milt Goodman invited us out on their lovely yacht for carol ship night.

That night Margie took Betty aside and I overheard her ask, "How's Margaret's love life?"

Betty told her that I was not doing that well on my own. Betty said that she and Art were surprised because I had been independent for so many years before meeting Ted. Margie thought for a bit and then said, "What's the matter with you, Betty, with such a nice man at May Taylor's party next door?"

Betty persuaded Art to phone Denny, May's son, who invited us to the party. Colin, his dad, was divorced from May, but they were still on good terms.

Well, I think it was magic. A girl, who had been sitting on a sofa next to Colin, got up to make room for me beside him. In a room full of strangers, we were holding hands almost right away. We did not stay too long, but on New Year's Eve Colin phoned from Whistler and asked me if I would go to dinner with him when he came back to town. I was flattered but I was leaving to go back to Florida. In the course of the conversation I said, "Have you ever been to Florida?"

Colin said "No."

So I said, "You should come down."

After I had been back in Englewood a few days, he phoned me and announced he was coming to see me. I was very excited, telling him I'd meet his plane in Sarasota. I reserved a table for dinner in a lovely restaurant on the water. The maitre d' asked me if I wanted candles and I said, "Of course. And please, a nice table with a view."

By this time I wasn't even sure what Colin looked like, because, as I said, we were only talking for an hour or so that night at the Christmas party in the Cove. I didn't learn until Colin came to Florida, that the party was at his first wife's place. I phoned my sister and she said that he was good looking with dark wavy hair with a little gray in it.

Colin and me.

I drove from Englewood to Sarasota, butterflies in my stomach but happy, knowing I'd soon see Colin again. I was staying that night with friends who invited me to bring Colin back to stay after our dinner.

Wouldn't you know it? It was pouring buckets when he arrived. He said, "Just like Vancouver!"

Colin was smart. He wore the

same brown suede jacket he had on when I met him and I recognized him right away.

We had just a marvellous time in the next few days. Colin came back to Englewood with me and we went to Disney World, Edison's home in Fort Myers, and into an everglade park. There are so many things to see and do in Florida and Colin said he was having the time of his life.

In the middle of his stay, a girl friend from Nova Scotia arrived for a visit. Billie had lost her husband recently and was going through a difficult time learning to carry on her life without him. I could understand so well how she was feeling. She and her husband, Walter, were our great friends in the Maritime Seniors Golf Association and we had often visited back and forth when our husbands were alive. Now, Billie and I would go shopping and do 'girl' things like having our hair done and enjoying coffee and a gossip while we were out together. Colin was quite happy to let us shop and gab while he amused himself. Billie stayed two weeks. Colin stayed for about five. I hated to see him go, but I knew I would see him again. After he arrived back in Vancouver he phoned me at least twice a week.

Then, the first part of April I was hit by my first tornado. It came roaring down one night and I never was so scared. It ripped the limbs of a large pine tree in my front yard and dumped them on my front door. Then it tore through the pool area, dumped all my lovely plants in the pool and the tore off the screen doors. Colin had made me a nice stand for my orchids and they were all a mess. It even ripped tiles off the roof. It sounded just like a freight train. I am sure I would have been killed if I had been in the pool area.

Colin phoned me that morning and I immediately started to cry. Poor guy! He thought he had said something wrong. Of course, he didn't know about the tornado. I said, "You should see the place. It's just a wreck." He tried to get me to stop crying but I was so happy to hear from him. Anyway, he said he missed me so much. So he proposed over the telephone and said he wanted to marry me. I said, "Yes". He said he would phone me the next day and hoped I would feel a little better.

The damage was devastating. I did not know where to start. The neighbours that weren't hurt by it helped me and the city sent out work crews, also. They hauled all the broken branches away, cleaned up the lawn and the mess off the roof. Colin phoned the first thing the next morning to see if I was all right. He said he was sorry he wasn't with me to help me with the mess. He also said, "I have a good idea. Why don't you come up in May and we will be married and go to Hawaii for a month?"

I remember thinking there must be guardian angels after all and replied, "Oh Colin, you really are an angel!" I'm sure he never guessed I meant it, quite literally.

My mind was in quite a state, with so many things

to take care of. I phoned my sister the same day to tell her that Colin and I were going to be married. This time, Betty and Arthur were delighted at the news. They said they would arrange for the wedding at St. Stephen's Church in Deep Cove, just down the road. They would send out the invitations and take care of the reception.

In Florida I was busy shopping for a wedding dress, my fourth! I did have clothes for Hawaii, as Florida is warm but I needed a new suit. I didn't think it could happen but I was on cloud nine again. It is magical when you meet someone who cares for you and you want to care for him or her, too. And there were no doubts about Colin. He was well known and respected in the Deep Cove community.

This time, Colin, instead of Betty and Art, met me at the airport. He had made reservations at the Tea House, at Ferguson Point, in Stanley Park. It is a lovely old restaurant where the service and food are first class and the view, out over the inlet and across to Vancouver Island is spectacular and romantic. Colin knew it was a favourite place of mine. I remember we had oysters on the half shell followed by the most wonderful poached salmon. Colin did all the ordering, including the wine, a British Columbian Riesling, and we shared a superb dessert, fresh fruit in a meringue shell topped with whipped cream. It was a truly romantic feast and, for the first time in two years, I felt safe and at ease. I knew I could trust Colin.

After dinner we drove across the Lions' Gate Bridge to see Colin's house in Edgemont Village, before driving me to Betty and Art's place in Deep Cove.

"Why Colin," I exclaimed when I stepped out of his car. "You love gardening, too!"

"I love the new gardener, better," he laughed.

It was the beginning of a great gardening partnership. We eventually sold Colin's home and moved, first to a model home opposite the Seymour Golf and Country Club, then to a townhouse in West Vancouver and finally, to the beautiful home in the British Properties where I live to this day. We designed lovely gardens in both places, spending happy hours digging, planting, watering and maintaining them. I was no stranger to the hard grunt work of gardening. In the past I'd picked up hammer, shovel, paintbrush or whatever tool I needed to do the job. I'm grateful that my father thought girls could do anything that boys could do.

I was very tired and could have slept for a week but, the next morning, which dawned sunny and beautiful as only Vancouver can be when it's not raining, there was a lot to do. Colin was such a thoughtful man. He said, "I want you to have a day's rest, Margaret, before I take you up to my place at Whistler."

He wanted to show me the chalet he built there. When he finished it, his daughter, Lynn, took it over and he was very proud of it. While we were there, he cooked me a meal, the first and only one he had ever cooked. I think it was a quiche and I was very impressed with his cooking talents. But, I'm almost certain that Lynn had made the quiche.

We were married on the 29th of May, 1982. It was a very beautiful day. Betty and Arthur's garden was gorgeous. Everything went well and we flew off to Hawaii. We stayed a couple of nights at the Royal Hawaiian, then flew over to Kauai to Colin's son Dennis and Mary's place. What a perfect spot, right on the ocean! The bay has a small, warm lagoon where turtles play in one corner. The sunsets and sunrises are, to use my grandson's favourite word, awesome. And, I never tire of watching the ocean. We hired a car and went all over the island. We were in paradise!

Chapter 28

The Cruising Life

I have never been on a cruise I did not enjoy, but some cruises have certainly been better than others. The one that stands out in my mind was a cruise I took with Colin in 1982.

I had flown to Vancouver to marry him, leaving my car at home in Florida. We decided that a nice way to travel back to Florida when we returned from our honeymoon in Hawaii was to take a repositioning cruise from Vancouver through the Panama Canal on the *SS Statendam* of the Holland America Line. We didn't know at the time that this was her last trip and the last time she would be calling at many ports. It was Colin's first cruise and it was a joy to see the fun he was having. When the ship went through the Panama Canal, he was entranced.

Back then, we could have guests on board. It was my new son in law Brett's birthday so we had a party with cake and champagne for him before we left port. As we left, we had paper streamers to throw ashore and the Vancouver Police Department Band played *Auld Lang Syne* as we sailed out of the harbour.

On the dock before boarding, our neighbours introduced us to Kay and Deed Saunders. A charming couple, they shared our enjoyment for dancing and we went together on the sight seeing trips in the ports along the way.

Our birthday party for Brett was the first of many on that cruise. Because it was the ship's final cruise, there were many parties with prizes at each. You just had to turn around and you won a bottle of champagne.

The most fun was the costume party. We were to come as a song title. In a big box with bolts of material and props, I found some mauve taffeta silk that had a few water stains on it. With a needle and thread, I fashioned it into a beautifully full skirt and pinned artificial flowers on it. Colin found a bowler hat and, wearing a gray waistband, he was Henry Higgins to my Eliza Dolittle. We won first prize!

Usually, Colin was a shy man everywhere but on the dance floor. Then he lost all his bashfulness and was even willing to lead me out on to the floor for the first dance. On the cruise, because he felt no one knew him, he relaxed and felt at ease.

Part of a cruise is getting yourself to the ship in the first place. This generally means a flight, often a long one. The worst time I ever had was flying to Greece to meet a Mediterranean cruise. Instead of flying directly to London for a change over to fly to Greece, we flew to

Toronto for a three-hour wait and then on to London for a twelve hour lay over. When we finally arrived in Greece, after being in transit almost thirty hours, we couldn't board the ship until the wee hours of the morning. We were too tired to unpack. The second night out is usually the captain's dinner and it wasn't until the next day that I discovered I had left my evening dress behind at the cleaner's.

Because of the delay, we missed a day in Athens and our first table mates on that cruise were odd and wouldn't talk to us. Fortunately, they moved and from then on we sat with a much more pleasant couple from California. However, smog was very thick in the Mediterranean, Rome was packed with tourists like ourselves and heavy rains met us in Gibraltar. This was the worst cruise I ever took.

Everyone talks about the food on cruises. The food is marvelous and there is plenty of it. Anyone should be able to find food they like, even those on special diets. When folks complain about the food, I tend to think that they do not cook themselves. I'm a good cook and I always enjoy the food on a cruise. My only complaint about the food is that there is too much of it. The cruise lines serve such big portions, that one cannot eat it all. I hate to waste food but I have learned to leave it on my plate if the servings are too generous. The chefs are very creative, making flowers and animals from vegetables and fruit. Their displays are gorgeous and the chefs on some cruises will even teach you this art.

I like to go to the dining room and be waited on. One of the reasons so many women like a cruise is that it is a complete holiday from cooking and housework. If you want to sleep in and miss breakfast, you can go up to the Lido where the chefs will usually make you an omelet

I usually ask for a table of eight as one can usually find someone in a large group with whom you can find a conversational meeting ground. The seatings are only for evening meals. You can also have a dinner up top or served in your room if you prefer.

Dressing for dinner was a custom I enjoyed but that has changed on cruises, and not for the better. I am of the old school and like to tidy up after the day's trip ashore, ping pong or golf game. It was fun to dress up on the formal night and both Ted and Colin loved wearing a tuxedo or white dinner jacket. I regret that folks are so casual now, with shirts hanging out and even coming to dinner in baseball caps. The staff attempt to enforce some basic rules but it is pretty hard to say, "I'm sorry, but you can't come in." There are so many cruise ships and competition is so high for bookings. I no longer worry about what someone else is wearing or not wearing. I'm just going to be myself.

Freighter travel was wonderful but it is not in the same category as cruising. For one thing, it is much more casual. Most of the time you wear shorts or slacks although I always dressed for dinner. I travelled on three freighter lines; the Moore-McCormack with 12 passengers, the Grace Line, a fruit ship with 52 passengers and the American Export Line. It had 96 passengers and everyone did dress for dinner. Two good ships were the *SS Monroe* and the *SS President Grant*.

One needs more time than money for freighter travel because the ships don't always follow the route you expect and there are delays. I think you must like to read, play bridge or take some needlework and to enjoy your own company on these ships. They would not take us when we were over seventy but with improved travel insurance that policy may have changed since I last travelled on a freighter. I highly recommend freighter travel.

Afterword

Betty and I saw my brother Jack only one more time, for a family reunion in Invermere. His wife died in her sleep several years ago. He had two daughters and a son. One of his daughters was mentally ill. We kept in touch and I tried to help her out from time to time. In the end, life became too much of a burden to her. She took her own life.

My dear stepdaughter, Eileen died of cancer last winter. I loved her dearly, and miss her very much.

Colin's family welcomed me as one of their own. I see them often and they always include me in family gatherings. Thanks to them, I have children and grandchildren now.

Betty has Alzheimer's, a cruel disease which makes her anxious as well as taking her memories away. She still paints, though. Until recently, she lived in her own home with assistance from caregivers. She is now in extended care. It breaks my heart to see her there but she could no longer live at home safely.

Recently I returned to visit the home our father built

in New Westminster. It had not changed at all since Father, Mother, Betty, Jack and I lived there so many years ago. You could still see Father's hand in the garden although the goldfish ponds have long since disappeared.

I live a full and active life, enjoying my home and garden, still travelling when the spirit moves me, and still a romantic. However, after Colin died I knew I would never marry again. Four husbands should be enough for anyone. I married to two of the best.

A return to our home in New Westminster.

Betty and Margaret with their prize-winning blooms.
Reprinted courtesy of Pacific Press.

ISBN 155395694-X

9 781553 956945